Schaum's Quick Guide
to Writing Great Research Papers

Forthcoming titles:

Schaum's Quick Guide to Writing Great Research Papers

Laurie Rozakis, Ph.D.
The State University of New York
College of Technology at Farmingdale

McGraw-Hill

New York   San Francisco   Washington, D.C.   Auckland   Bogotá
Caracas   Lisbon   London   Madrid   Mexico City   Milan
Montreal   New Delhi   San Juan   Singapore
Sydney   Tokyo   Toronto

Library of Congress Cataloging-in-Publication Data

Rozakis, Laurie.
    Schaum's quick guide to writing great research papers / Laurie
Rozakis.
        p.   cm. — (Schaum's quick guide series)
    Includes index.
    ISBN 0-07-012300-4
    1. Report writing.   2. Research.   I. Title.   II. Series.
LB1047.3.R69   1999
808'.02—dc21   99-13669
                                                                    CIP

McGraw-Hill

A Division of The McGraw-Hill Companies

6 7 8 9 0   DOC/DOC   0 3

ISBN 0-07-012300-4

*The sponsoring editor for this book was Barbara Gilson, the editing supervisor was Fred
Dahl, the designer was Inkwell Publishing Services, and the production supervisor was
Sherri Souffrance. It was set in Stone Serif by Inkwell Publishing Services.*

Printed and bound by R. R. Donnelley & Sons Company.

Contents

Schaum's Quick Guide
to Writing Great Research Papers

Part I

Getting Started

Chapter 1

What Is a Research Paper?

Research is a way of life dedicated to discovery.

ANONYMOUS

Few of us are ever going to become professional researchers, but *all* of us will find times when research is indispensable to our lives. Whether you're looking for information about a car's safety record, a community's schools, or a company's stock, you'll need to know how to gather, sort, and track the facts and opinions available to you.

That's why you need to know how to do a research paper. A research paper is such a useful and efficient method for gathering and presenting reliable information that preparing one is frequently assigned in high schools and colleges. In addition, research papers are often important in business, especially in fast changing fields where facts and opinions must be sorted. These businesses include law, manufacturing, retailing, security, fashion, computer technology, banking, insurance, and accounting.

Research Papers vs. Term Papers

A *research paper* and its first cousin, the *term paper*, are often confused. In part, that's because there are no fixed differences between them regarding length, topic, format, or citations. If you held a research paper in one hand and a term paper in the other without reading them for content, they would *appear* to be the same.

Nonetheless, the two forms of written communication are *not* the same, as a closer examination reveals. Let's look at each type of essay to see how they are the same and different.

A *research paper* presents and argues a *thesis*, the writer's proposition or opinion. It is an analytical or persuasive essay that evaluates a position. As such, a research paper tries to convince readers that the writer's argument is valid or at least deserves serious consideration.

As a result, a research paper requires the writer to be creative in using facts, details, examples, and opinions to support a point. The writer has to be original and inventive in deciding which facts best support the thesis and which ones are superfluous.

When you write a research paper, you have to read what authorities have written about the topic and then write an essay in which you draw your own conclusions about the topic. Since your thesis is fresh and original, you can't merely summarize what someone else has written. Instead, you have to synthesize information from many different sources to create something that is your own.

A *term paper*, in contrast, is a collection of facts. It does not argue a point; it does not try to persuade readers to think or act a certain way. Since a term paper is a summary of information from one or more sources, you are merely reporting what others have said. This is not to say that a term paper doesn't have many valid uses. For example, it is very helpful for people who need a great deal of data in a condensed, easy-to-read form. Government workers are often asked to prepare term papers with information on weather, transportation, economics, and so forth.

Differences between a Research Paper and a Term Paper	
Research Paper	**Term Paper**
Argues a point.	Presents data.
Formulates a thesis.	Reports what others said.
Is argumentative/persuasive.	Is expository/descriptive.
Evaluates.	Summarizes.
Considers *why* and *how*.	Considers *what*.

Examples:

Here is how typical college-level topics could be developed for research papers and term papers.

Topic: Baseball

Research Paper
There should/should not be interleague play.

Term Paper
The history of baseball

Topic: Testing

Research Paper
Standardized tests are/are not an accurate measure of success in college.

Term Paper
Different types of standardized tests

Topic: School

Research Paper
Year-round school will/will not raise students' achievement.

Term Paper
Survey of topics taught in secondary schools

Topic: Thomas Hardy

Research Paper
Hardy is/is not the greatest English novelist of his era.

Term Paper
Chronology of Hardy's life and writing

What Are the Qualities of a Good Research Paper?

No matter what its topic or length, an effective research paper meets the following ten criteria:

1. The paper has a clear thesis.
2. The writer shows a strong understanding of the topic and source material used.
3. There is evidence that the writer has read widely on the topic, including the recognized authorities in the field.
4. The paper acknowledges the opposition but shows why the point being argued is more valid.
5. The points are organized in a clear and logical way.

6. Each point is supported by solid, persuasive facts and examples.

7. Every outside source is carefully documented.

8. All supporting material can be verified.

9. The paper follows the standard conventions of the genre, including the use of correct documentation and a Works Cited page.

10. The paper uses standard written English. This is the level of diction and usage expected of educated people in high schools, colleges, universities, and work settings.

Time Management

Whether you are writing a research paper as a class assignment or as part of a work-related assignment, the odds are very good that you are not going to have all the time you want. In nearly every case, you are working against a deadline. You have to produce a paper of a certain length by a certain date.

Since you are working under pressure within narrow constraints, it's important to know how to allocate your time from the very beginning. In fact, one of the most challenging aspects of writing a paper is planning your time effectively. You don't want to end up spending the night before the paper is due cramming material in the library and typing until you're bleary-eyed. Your paper will not be very successful—and you'll be wiped out for days.

No one deliberately plans to leave work to the last minute, but few novice writers (and even some more experienced ones!) realize how much time it takes to select a topic, find information, read and digest it, take notes, and write successive drafts of the paper. This is especially true when you're faced with all the other pressures of school and work. No one can produce a good research paper without adequate time.

That's why it's crucial to allocate your time carefully from the day you get the assignment. Before you plunge into the process, start by making a plan. Here are some plans to get you started.

Each plan assumes a five-day workweek, so you can relax on the weekends.

The last step is always "wiggle room." When it comes to any major project such as a research paper, things often go wrong. Perhaps the book you really need is out of the library and it will take too long to get it from another library. So you have to rely more heavily on other sources, which means more time doing research than you had counted on. Or maybe you lost some of your bibliography cards, the dog ate your rough draft, your hard drive crashed.

Examples:

4-Week Plan (20 Days)

Task	Time
1. Selecting a topic	1/2 day
2. Narrowing the topic	1/2 day
3. Crafting a thesis statement	1/2 day
4. Doing preliminary research	2 days
5. Taking notes	2 days
6. Creating an outline	1/2 day
7. Writing the first draft	3 days
8. Finding additional sources	2 days
9. Integrating source materials	1 day
10. Using internal documentation	1/2 day
11. Creating a Works Cited page	1/2 day
12. Writing front matter/end matter	1 day
13. Revising, editing, proofreading	3 days
14. Keyboarding	1 day
15. Wiggle room	2 days

6-Week Plan (30 Days)

Task	Time
1. Selecting a topic	1 day
2. Narrowing the topic	1 day
3. Crafting a thesis statement	1 day
4. Doing preliminary research	3 days
5. Taking notes	3 days
6. Creating an outline	1 day

7. Writing the first draft	4 days
8. Finding additional sources	3 days
9. Integrating source materials	2 days
10. Using internal documentation	1 day
11. Creating a Works Cited page	1 day
12. Writing front matter/end matter	1 day
13. Revising, editing, proofreading	4 days
14. Keyboarding	2 days
15. Wiggle room	2 days

8-Week Plan (40 Days)

Task	Time
1. Selecting a topic	2 days
2. Narrowing the topic	2 days
3. Crafting a thesis statement	1 day
4. Doing preliminary research	4 days
5. Taking notes	5 days
6. Creating an outline	1 day
7. Writing the first draft	7 days
8. Finding additional sources	3 days
9. Integrating source materials	3 days
10. Using internal documentation	2 days
11. Creating a Works Cited page	1 day
12. Writing front matter/end matter	1 day
13. Revising, editing, proofreading	4 days
14. Keyboarding	2 days
15. Wiggle room	2 days

12-Week Plan (60 Days)

If you have 12 weeks (60 days) to complete a research paper, remember that longer is not necessarily better! With a long lead time, it's mighty tempting to leave the assignment to the last minute. After all, you do have *plenty* of time. But "plenty of time" has a way of evaporating fast. In many instances, it's actually easier to have less time in which to write a research paper, because you know that you're under pressure to produce.

Now that you've been warned about the "time trap," if you have 12 weeks (60 days) in which to complete a research paper, here's how to use it.

1. Selecting a topic   3 days
2. Narrowing the topic   2 days
3. Crafting a thesis statement   1 day
4. Doing preliminary research   8 days
5. Taking notes   8 days
6. Creating an outline   2 days
7. Writing the first draft   10 days
8. Finding additional sources   4 days
9. Integrating source materials   3 days
10. Using internal documentation   2 days
11. Creating a Works Cited page   1 day
12. Writing front matter/end matter 2 days
13. Revising, editing, proofreading 6 days
14. Keyboarding   3 days
15. Wiggle room   5 days

Now that we've gotten a toe wet, it's time to learn how to select a topic. This is covered in the next chapter.

Chapter 2

How Do I Select a Subject?

*Writing is no trouble: you just jot down ideas as they
occur to you. The* jotting *is simplicity itself—it is the
occurring which is difficult.*

STEPHEN LEACOCK

Here, There, and Everywhere

This book presents a clear, effective, proven way to write a
fine research paper. The steps are arranged in chronological
order, from start to finish. Be aware, however, that writers
rarely take such neat steps. While it is strongly recommend-
ed that you follow the steps in order, don't worry if you find
yourself repeating a step, doing two steps at the same time,
or skipping a step and then returning to it.

For example, you select and narrow your topic to create
a thesis statement. Then you set off to find the information
you need. Once you start looking at sources, however, you
discover that there is (a) too much material on the topic or
(b) not enough. In this case, you might go back to the previous step and rework your thesis to accommodate your findings and the new direction your work has taken. (Of course,
you always have the option of sticking with your original
thesis and creating the research material you need. More on
this in Chapter 7.)

Here's another common occurrence. You think you have found all the material you need and so have started writing. But half-way through your first draft, you find that you are missing a key piece of information, a crucial fact, an essential detail. To plug the hole, you go back and find the material—even though you are, in effect, repeating a step in the process. That's OK.

The process presented in this book is effective, but remember that "one size may not fit all." As a result, you may find yourself adapting the information here to fit your particular writing style.

That said, let's move on to the first step in the process of writing a research paper, selecting a topic.

Step 1: Brainstorming Subjects

Sometimes, your teacher, professor, or supervisor assigns the subject for your research paper. In these cases, you usually have very little choice about what you will write. You *may* be able to stretch the subject a bit around the edges or tweak it to fit your specific interests, but most often you have to follow the assignment precisely as it was given. To do otherwise means risking failure, since the instructor was precise in the assignment.

In other cases, however, you are instructed to develop the subject and topic on your own. Very often this is part of the research paper process, for it teaches you to generate ideas and evaluate them. It helps you learn valuable decision-making skills in addition to writing and research methods.

Choosing a subject for a research paper calls for good judgment and solid decision-making skills. Experienced writers know that the success or failure of a research paper often depends on its subject; even the best writers find it difficult (if not impossible) to create a winning paper around an unsuitable subject.

The right topic can make your paper; the wrong one can break it. Unsuitable subjects share one or more of the following characteristics:

- They cannot be completed within the time allocated.
- They cannot be researched since the material does not exist.
- They do not persuade since they are expository or narrative.
- They are inappropriate, offensive, or vulgar.

Nearly every subject *can* be researched, but not every subject *should* be researched for a number of reasons. For example, why bother researching a subject that many others have done before you? Trite, shopworn, and boring subjects often lead to trite, shopworn, and boring research papers. Give yourself a break by starting with a fresh, exciting subject.

As a result, it's important to think through a subject completely before you rush into research and writing. In addition, your writing will be better if your subject is suitable for your readers and purpose.

PLANNING

Where can you get ideas for research paper subjects? You have two main sources: *yourself* or *outside experts.*

Yourself

Let's start with yourself. All writing begins with thinking. When you come up with a subject for a research paper, as with any other writing assignment, you must draw on yourself as a source. All writers depend on their storehouse of experience—everything they have seen, heard, read, and even dreamed.

People often worry that they have nothing to write about, especially when it comes to a mammoth project such as a research paper. Often, however, you know far more than you are willing to give yourself credit for. Your task? Discover which of your ideas is most suitable for the research paper you have to do.

Here are some proven techniques for generating subjects. Since not every method works for every writer, experiment with these techniques to find the one or ones that suit your writing style. And even if one method works very well for you, don't be afraid to try other ones. They may uncover still other possible subjects for your paper.

1. **Keep an idea book.** Many professional writers keep an "idea book" as a place to store their ideas and let them incubate. Think of this as a scrapbook rather than as a diary or journal.

   Examples:
   Your idea book can include:
   Newspaper clippings.
   Magazine articles.
   Personal letters that may spark ideas.
   Snapshots.
   Postcards.
   Other visuals that can serve as the seeds for a great research paper.

2. **Listing.** You can list all the ideas you associate with a specific subject. This method allows you to come up with many ideas fast because you are writing words, not sentences or paragraphs. Jot down the numbers 1 to 10, and then list any ideas you have for research paper subjects.

   Example:
   1. Restricting immigration
   2. Celebrity worship
   3. Eating disorders
   4. Sport utility vehicles
   5. Women in the military
   6. Working women
   7. Divorce laws
   8. Censorship of novels
   9. Euthanasia
   10. Gays in the military

3. **Webbing (clustering).** *Webbing,* also called *clustering* or *mapping,* is a visual way of sparking ideas for subjects. Since a web looks very different from a paragraph or list, many writers find that it frees their mind to roam over a wider variety of ideas.

   When you create a web, first write your subject in the center of a page. Draw a circle around it. Next draw lines radiating from the center and circles at the end of each line. Write an idea in each circle.

Example:

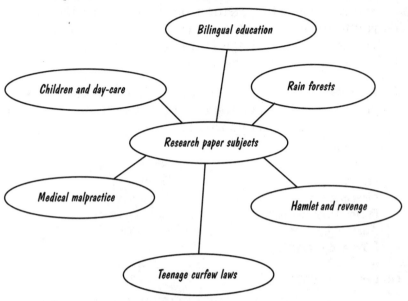

4. **Making visuals.** A web is a visual format, but you can use other visuals to generate ideas for research paper subjects. Charts work especially well for some people, blanks and word balloons for others. Experiment with different visual formats until you find which ones work best for you in each writing situation.

Example:
Webs work well with humanities-based topics.

5. **5 Ws and H.** The "5 Ws and H" stand for *who, what, when, where, why,* and *how.* They are also called "The Journalist's Questions" because they appear in the first paragraph (the "lead") of every news story. Asking these questions forces you to approach a subject from several different angles. Many people find this approach useful for starting highly detailed papers.

6. **Freewriting.** This is nonstop writing that jogs your memory and releases hidden ideas. When you freewrite, jot down whatever comes to mind. Don't worry about

spelling, punctuation, grammar, or style. Just try to keep writing. Select the method of composition that allows you to freewrite most quickly: keyboarding or longhand. The key to freewriting is letting your mind roam and seeing what subjects it uncovers.

7. **Reading.** Reading widely can help you come up with great research paper topics. Try different genres to get ideas. Don't restrict yourself!

   Examples:

Short stories	Novels
Essays	Poems
Newspapers	Magazines
Professional journals	Critical reviews
Autobiographies	Biographies
Plays and drama	Scripts

OUTSIDE EXPERTS

Can't come up with anything you like? Why not consult outside experts? In addition to speaking to people who have written research papers, check with the teachers, parents, and professionals you know. Doctors, lawyers, accountants, real estate salespeople, computer programmers, and other businesspeople are all excellent sources for ideas.

Step 2: Considering Your Parameters

If you are asked to develop your own subject for a research paper, how can you decide which of the subjects you have brainstormed shows the most promise? Start with these four guidelines:

1. **Time.** The amount of time you have to write influences every writing situation, but especially a research paper. Since so many research-related variables are out of your control—such as availability of materials— you have to select a subject that you can complete in the time allotted. This is not easy to determine when you first start

writing research papers, however. For help, study the sample papers in the last section of this guide.

2. **Length.** The length of the paper is also a factor in your choice of topics. It obviously takes much longer to write a 50-page research paper than to write a 10-page research paper. Weigh this consideration as you select a subject. The shorter the paper and the longer the time you have to write, the more leeway you have to select a challenging subject.

3. **Research.** The type of research you use also determines the subject you select. For instance, if your assignment specifies that you must use primary sources such as letters, interviews, and eyewitness accounts, you might not wish to do a paper on Shakespeare, since relatively few primary sources are available and they are difficult to read. Conversely, if your teacher has specified that you may use secondary sources such as critical reviews, a paper on one of Shakespeare's plays would be very suitable.

4. **Sources.** The number of sources you must use and their availability is also a factor in your choice of a subject. If you have access to a major university library with a million or more volumes, you are probably going to find the material you need. But if you do not have an extensive library in your area, it might be much harder for you to get secondary material. In this case, you might want to consider a subject that requires more primary sources such as experiments, interviews, and surveys. See Chapter 5 for a full discussion of primary and secondary sources.

Step 3: Evaluating Subjects

You should not select a subject hastily, but neither should you "shop till you drop"! Here are ten guidelines to make the process easier:

1. **Consider your purpose.** With a research paper, your purpose is to convince. Persuasive writing succeeds in large part because it has such a clear sense of purpose. Keep your purpose in mind as you weigh the suitability

of various subjects. If you cannot slant the subject to be persuasive, it is not a good choice for a research paper.

2. **Select a subject you like.** If you have a choice, try to select a subject that interests you. Since you will be working with the subject for weeks and even months, you will find writing your research paper much more enjoyable if you like the subject matter.

   Start with hobbies, sports, favorite courses, career plans, and part-time jobs.

   Example:
   If you are interested in computers, you might want to:
   Look behind the scenes at programming, hardware, or systems analysis.
   Evaluate the impact of computers on specific fields.
   Consider the effect of computers on children. (Should kids be playing outside with their friends rather than spending so much time at a keyboard? Are we raising a generation of sedentary children as a result of an overemphasis on computer skills?)

   School courses can also be an excellent source of topics for your research paper. If your favorite class is physical education, consider a persuasive paper related to the subject.

   Example:
   Should physical education be mandatory?
   On the other side, should more time be allocated to physical education—up to two or even three hours a day?
   Is there a relationship between physical and emotional health?
   Can being physically fit have an impact on our emotional health?

   What happens if you have been assigned a subject you detest? See if you can find a slant—an aspect of the subject—that you like.

3. **Be practical.** Even though you want a subject that appeals to you, look for topics that have sufficient information available, but not so much information that you can't possibly wade through it all.

   Example:
   Avoid sweeping papers on the entire tax system, transportation methods, or computers. You'll be writing long past the mandatory retirement age.

Writing a research paper is challenging enough without making the task that much harder for yourself.

4. **Beware of "hot" subjects.** "Hot" subjects—very timely, popular issues—often lack the expert attention that leads to reliable information. The books, articles, and interviews on such subjects have often been produced in great haste. As a result, they are not carefully fact-checked. In addition, such research papers get stale *very* quickly; sometimes the issue can seem dated even before you finish writing the paper!

   The media, especially newspapers, magazines, radio shows, and web sites, *can* be an excellent source of research paper subjects. But rather than focusing on the side everyone else sees, probe a little deeper for the story behind the story. This can help you avoid getting trapped in a subject that's here today but gone tomorrow.

5. **Consider your audience.** As you select a subject, always focus on your *audience*—the person or people who will be reading your paper. Don't select a subject that condescends to your readers, offends them, or panders to them. Don't try to shock them, either: It always backfires.

6. **Recognize that not all questions have answers.** When you write a research paper, you are attempting to find an answer to the question you have posed or the one given to you. Remember that not all research questions lead to definitive answers. Rather, some questions invite informed opinions based on the evidence you have gathered from research. Dealing with questions that don't have definitive answers can make your paper provocative and intriguing.

   Now that you've learned how to select a subject, we'll turn to the crucial issue of narrowing your topic. You'll learn why this is such an important step in a successful paper.

Chapter 3

How Do I Narrow My Topic? (and Why?)

*Writing is just having a sheet of paper, a pen, and not
a shadow of an idea of what you're going to say.*

FRANÇOISE SAGAN

The real challenge in dealing with research paper topics comes when you choose or are assigned a subject that is very broad. How can you deal with this? You have to *narrow the subject into a topic*. This means you find smaller aspects of the topic within the subject area to use as the basis of your research paper.

Fortunately, nearly all very broad topics can be subdivided in hundreds of ways. And just as luckily, you only have to think of a few subtopics until you come to one that seems the best choice for your research paper.

Subject vs. Topic

Let's start by reviewing the difference between a subject and a topic.

SUBJECTS

A *subject* of a research paper is the general content. Subjects are broad and general.

Examples of subjects for a research paper:

Health
Music
Television
Education
The Civil War
Travel
Athletics
Video games
Ecology
Foreign policy

TOPICS

The *topic* of a research paper is the specific issue discussed.

Examples of topics based on the previous subjects:

Subject	Topic
Health	Increasing/decreasing AIDS funding
	AIDS testing of health care workers
	The benefits of fad diets
Music	Censorship of rap music
	Links between music and violence
	Comparison of two singers, groups, etc.
Television	The V-chip in televisions
	The cable wars
	A specific show or series
Education	Year-round schooling
	Changes in the curriculum
	Weapons policies
The Civil War	Decisive battles
	Key generals
Travel	Airplane safety
	Specific destinations
	Solo travelers
Athletics	Status of "amateurs" in athletics
	Funding of women in sports
	Sports and advertising

World Wide Web	"Filtering" on-line sources
	Ordering from on-line companies
	Virtual romances—a real danger?
Ecology	Wetlands vs. mini-malls
	Saving endangered species
	Recycling—worth the effort?
Foreign policy	America's stand on the establishment of a Palestinian state

Shaping Your Ideas

Every time you narrow a subject into a topic, remember your boundaries and parameters: time, length, audience, and purpose. Keep all other special considerations in mind as well. Always consider what you can handle within the restrictions you have been given—as well as what you would most enjoy writing about for several months!

1. Start with a general subject that interests you and fits the parameters of the assignment.
2. Phrase the subject as a question.
3. Brainstorm subdivisions of the subject to create topics.
4. Consult different sources for possible subtopics, such as the card catalog, reference books, magazines, friends, and the media.
5. Sift the ideas until you find one that suits your taste and the assignment.
6. Write your final topic as a question.

   That said, let's explore the process one writer followed to narrow a subject into a topic.

Example:
Samantha wanted to write a research paper on some aspect of television, a very broad subject.

By looking through the card catalog, talking to friends, watching television, and reading articles on the subject in general interest news magazines, Samantha came up with these ideas:

Subject	Television
Question	What do I want to find out about TV?
Specific topics	TV as "vast wasteland"
	TV as "chewing gum for the mind"
	Children and television
	Educational television
	Cable television
	Television documentaries
	Golden Age of television
	Television and ethnic stereotypes
	Sex and violence on television
	Amount of TV watched and its effect
	Tabloid TV

Reading over the list, Samantha realized that some of her ideas were still very broad. For example, the idea of "children and television" is large enough to be the subject of a book—or a series of books! The same is true of "television documentaries," "Golden Age of television," and "cable television."

Even narrowing down some of these topics might not lead to persuasive essays. "Cable television," for instance, seems better suited to an expository essay that explains the history of the field, its impact on viewers, and so on.

One evening, Samantha was watching reruns of a children's "educational" television show she had loved years ago when the idea came to her: *Is educational television really educational?* Maybe educational TV indeed taught numbers, letters, and other necessary content— or perhaps it affected children negatively.

Now Samantha had her narrowed topic and could continue with the next step, writing a thesis statement. This is covered in the next chapter.

Further Examples:

Subject	Topic
Supreme Court	Is the Supreme Court more important than Congress in setting social policy?
Intelligence	Is intelligence determined by nature or nurture?

Sports	Are competitive sports, such as football and basketball, overemphasized in American culture?
Education	Does a college education necessarily prepare a student to obtain a well paying job? Should it serve this function?
Eating disorders	Are eating disorders, such as anorexia and bulimia, caused by the media's emphasis on appearance and weight?
Boating	Should all boaters be required to earn a license?

Checklist

Deciding on a suitable subject and narrowing it down to manageable proportions are crucial steps toward the success of your research paper. How can you decide if you have correctly narrowed your topic? Use this checklist every time you select a topic:

_____ 1. Is my topic *too* limited?

Problem: Sometimes in your zeal to make the topic more precise, you narrow it so much that you don't have enough left to write about.

Solution: Always remember how many pages you have to fill. The overly narrow topic may be just right for a 350- to 500-word essay; so save it for that assignment. Then find a topic that fills the length required by the research paper assignment.

_____ 2. Is my topic still *too* broad?

Problem: You may think you have narrowed your topic sufficiently, but it may still be too vast for the assignment.

Solution: Check your sources. How many pages do they devote to the topic? If it takes other writers a book to answer the question you have posed, your topic is still too big.

_____ 3. Is my topic too technical?

Problem: The topic you have selected is highly technical and you don't have the background to answer it.

Solution: Get a new topic. Unless you have the background you need for the topic, you're going to end up spending most of your time backpedaling and filling in the gaps in your knowledge. This is not the time to teach yourself nuclear physics, calculus, or computer programming in C+++.

_____ 4. Is my topic stale?

Problem: Everyone seems to know everything about your topic. Who wants to read another paper about the bad effects of alcohol, speeding, or street drugs? What reaction can you expect? Been there, done that, got the T-shirt. If your topic bores you before you've even started writing, you can bet it will bore your audience.

Solution: Get a new topic that is fresh and original. A sparkling topic automatically gives you an edge, even if your writing is a little weak.

_____ 5. Is my topic too controversial?

Problem: You are afraid you are going to offend your audience with a controversial topic such as abortion, unsealed adoption records, or sex education.

Solution: Don't take the risk. Start with a new topic that suits both your audience and purpose. Papers that shock and offend take unnecessary risks.

_____ 6. Is my topic not controversial at all?

Problem: If there's only one opinion about your topic or the vast majority of people think the same way as you do, there's no point in arguing the issue.

Solution: You can't argue two sides of the issue if your topic has only one side. Get a new topic that is controversial (without being offensive, of course!).

_____ 7. Is the topic too new?

Problem: If the topic is too fresh, such as the Starr Report, there may not be sufficient information available yet to fill a paper on your specific subtopics.

Solution: Find a topic that affords you sufficient information to cover the issue thoroughly.

_____ 8. Do I like my topic enough to want to write a research paper on it?

Problem: Your teacher likes your topic, your parents like your topic, your buddies like your topic. Even your dog likes your topic. The problem? *You* don't like your topic.

Solution: You guessed it: Get a new topic.

In Chapter 4, you'll explore how to write a thesis statement. That way, you'll learn how to keep your writing on target.

How Do I Write a Thesis Statement?

Writing is a deliberate act; one has to make up one's mind to do it.

JAMES BRITTON

What do you want to discover through your research? In what order will you present your ideas? An effective thesis statement is designed to answer these questions. That's why, once you've narrowed your topic, it's time to turn your attention to your *thesis statement,* which is the central point you're proving.

Requirements for a Thesis Statement

Here are the five basic requirements for a thesis statement:

1. It states the *topic* of the research paper, the main idea.
2. It shows the *purpose* of your essay; in this case, to persuade your readers that your point is valid and deserves serious consideration.
3. It shows the *direction* of your argument. As a result, a good thesis statement implies (or states) the order in which your ideas will be presented.

4. It is written in focused, *specific language*.
5. It is *interesting*, showing a clear voice and style.

Since your thesis statement is the backbone of your paper, spend the time to craft it exactly as you want and need it to be. Here's how to do that.

List Topics

What do you want to know about your subject? What questions do you want answered? Start by listing topics and possible subtopics.

Example:
Here's how one writer started writing a thesis statement for a research paper on the women's movement.

Topic	Contemporary women and work
Possible subtopics	High-quality education
	Appropriate training
	Pay gap between men and women
	Enormous progress in workforce
	Economic necessity for work
	Women and the "second shift"
	Women's traditional roles
	Women taking "men's jobs"
	Personal satisfaction from work
	Fight against discrimination
	The "glass ceiling"
	Personal ambition
	Restricted jobs/"women's work"
	"Pink-collar jobs"
	"White-collar jobs"
	"Blue-collar jobs"
	Sexual harassment on the job
	Sexual stereotypes about women
	Child care
	Women's movement

Don't be afraid to make your list too long, since your purpose at this point is to see how many subtopics you can generate. In addition, you don't know how much information you can get on each of these subtopics. As a result, this list includes specific details as well as broad topics.

By developing and refining your list of subtopics while forming your thesis statement, you won't lose time by having to double back later. But keep in mind that this is a first step; everything is carved in sand, not granite.

Having trouble? A number of computer software programs can help you with this step in your research paper. You may wish to try one and see if it suits your needs.

Draft a Thesis Statement

After you have narrowed your topic and drafted a list of ideas, you're ready to write a preliminary thesis statement. How can you turn this list of subtopics into a thesis statement?

1. Sort the ideas into categories.
2. Select the categories you want to use.
3. Formulate your thesis around these categories.
4. Write your thesis as a declarative sentence.
5. Be open to revision.

Follow this pattern:

[I expect to prove] an assertion about your topic.

Example:

Topic: Contemporary women and work

Training	**Discrimination**
High-quality education	The "glass ceiling"
Appropriate training	Pay gap between men and women
	"Pink-collar jobs"
	"White-collar jobs"
	"Blue-collar jobs"
	Women taking "men's jobs"
	Restricted jobs/"women's work"
	Sexual harassment on the job

Reasons Women Work	Pressures
Personal satisfaction	Women and the "second shift"
Economic necessity	Women's traditional roles
Ambition	Sexual stereotypes about women
	Child care

Tentative Thesis Statements

1. Women won't achieve true equality in the workforce until outmoded sexual stereotypes, discrimination, sexual harassment, and internal as well as external pressures are eliminated.
2. We've come a long way, baby, but women still face significant pressure and discrimination in the work force.
3. With quality education and training, female workers can overcome the discrimination and pressure they face in many jobs.
4. Despite pressure and discrimination, women have made great strides in the workforce.
5. The women's movement has been instrumental in eliminating much of the discrimination and harassment women face on the job.

Let's look at the first tentative thesis statement.

Example:

Women won't achieve true equality in the workforce until outmoded sexual stereotypes, discrimination, sexual harassment, and internal as well as external pressures are eliminated.

Thesis: Women have yet to achieve equality in the workforce.

Main points in order:

1. Discrimination must be eliminated.
2. Outmoded sexual stereotypes must be eliminated.
3. Sexual harassment must be eliminated.
4. Internal as well as external pressures must be eliminated.

Research may lead you to revise your thesis, even disprove it, but stating it up front points you in the direction of your investigation.

Sample Thesis Statements

Many writers use models to help them shape and evaluate their work. Here are some sample thesis statements that you can use as models for a paper of 7–10 pages. Compare these statements to the one you are writing.

Examples:

Too General	**On Target**
Rain forests are irreplaceable.	Rain forests must be preserved because they offer people many resources we cannot replace.
Too Narrow	**On Target**
Mothers Against Drunk Driving is an excellent program.	Some programs designed to eliminate drunk driving have been effective, but far more efforts are needed, especially concerning teenager drunk driving.
Too General	**On Target**
"The Yellow Wallpaper" is a great short story.	The wallpaper in "The Yellow Wallpaper" symbolizes the narrator's suffocating life.
Too Narrow	**On Target**
Bilingual education helps students maintain their native language.	Bilingual education should be continued because it preserves students' heritage as well as their native language.
Too General	**On Target**
Bilingual education isn't effective.	Bilingual education should be eliminated because it limits students' success, burdens students unfairly, and isn't cost-effective.
Too Narrow	**On Target**
A flat tax helps tax accountants.	A flat tax would benefit the government, business, and consumers.
Too General	**On Target**
The cafeteria isn't very good.	The cafeteria could attract more business if it improved the quality of its food, its appearance, and the attitude of the staff.

Check Your Work

Use this checklist to evaluate your thesis statement:

_____ 1. The thesis statement clearly states the main idea of my research paper.

_____ 2. The thesis statement indicates that I am writing a persuasive essay.

_____ 3. From the thesis statement, readers can see the order in which my ideas will be presented.

_____ 4. The thesis statement uses specific language rather than vague, general terms.

_____ 5. The thesis statement is interesting, lively, intriguing; it makes my audience want to read the entire paper.

_____ 6. If the thesis statement is in response to an assignment, it fulfills the requirements and meets the parameters.

_____ 7. The thesis statement is the appropriate scope for the assignment, neither too broad nor too general.

_____ 8. The thesis statement shows evidence of original thought and effort. The topic is fresh and worth my effort to write.

In this chapter, you found out how to write a thesis statement—and why! Stay tuned for the inside scoop on finding the information you need. It's all in Chapter 5.

Part II

Doing Research

How Can I Find the Information I Need?

The beginning of research is curiosity, its essence is discernment, and its goal is truth and justice.
Isaac H. Satanov

The Information Explosion

The information age is upon us—and there's no escape! Ready or not, we are living in the midst of the greatest explosion of information the world has ever seen. No other generation has been blitzed by the books, newspapers, magazines, journals, surveys, advertisements, videos, television shows, movies, maps, charts, graphs, CDs, and tapes that we encounter daily. And that doesn't take into account all the on-line sources, such as Web sites, electronic bulletin boards, newsgroups, and e-mail. More information has been produced in the last fifty years than in the previous five thousand.

Consider these facts about the amount of information available to us today:

- Fifty thousand books and ten thousand magazines are published every year in America alone.
- Every day, seven thousand scientific studies are written.

- *One* daily edition of *The New York Times* contains more information than an educated person in the sixteenth century absorbed in his or her entire life.

There is so much information that even the huge Library of Congress in Washington, D.C., fears the downpour. Currently, the library houses more than 100 million items. To deal with the onslaught of new information, the library has announced a plan to convert all the important information it contains into digital form. The new collection, called the "National Digital Library," will become the most extensive source of information for the National Information Infrastructure, the so-called "Information Superhighway."

Futurists predict that this onslaught of information will only increase. By the year 2000, the amount of information produced will double *every two years*.

What impact does this trend have on you as you prepare your research paper? All the information you need is probably available, but you must know how to locate and sort the useful facts from the useless ones. And with much out there, knowing how to do research can save you many frustrating hours in the library. Let's start this process by examining the different kinds of material you can find.

Primary and Secondary Sources

All research can be sorted into two categories: primary sources and secondary sources. It is important to know the distinction between these two types of sources because they affect how you gather research.

PRIMARY SOURCES

Primary sources are those created by *direct observation.* The writers were participants in or observers of the events they describe.

Examples:
Primary sources include:
Autobiographies.
Diaries.
Eyewitness accounts.

Interviews.
Historical records and documents.
Journals.
Letters.
Logs.
Oral histories.
Maps prepared by direct observation.
Photos taken at the scene.
Statistics.
Surveys.

SECONDARY SOURCES

Secondary sources are written by people with indirect knowledge. They rely on primary sources or other secondary sources for their information.

Examples:
Secondary sources include:
Abstracts.
Almanacs.
Biographies.
Book reviews.
Books written by nonparticipants.
Critical analyses.
Encyclopedias.
Explanations.
Government documents.
Indexes.
Interpretations.
Literary criticism.
Textbooks.

Primary sources are not necessarily better (or worse) than secondary sources.

Primary Sources:

- Provide facts and viewpoints that may not be available from other sources.

- Often have an immediacy and freshness that secondary sources lack.

- May be affected by the author's bias.

Secondary Sources:

- May offer a broader perspective than primary sources.
- Tend to be less immediate than primary sources.
- May be affected by the author's bias.

Effective research papers often use a mix of both primary and secondary sources.

Example:
A research paper on the history of comic books might include:

Primary sources, such as interviews with editors from the industry, artists, and writers.

Secondary sources, such as books, magazine articles, and newspaper articles on the subject.

You need to evaluate each source individually. This is covered in Chapter 10.

Some topics, in contrast, require one type of material more than the other.

Example:
A research paper on intelligence will likely use secondary sources; a paper on Vietnam, in contrast, might draw more on primary materials.

Basic Search Strategy

Before we get into how to use specific resources, let's cover the general guidelines for research. The following suggestions can make your task easier and less frustrating.

1. **Use key words.** Start by listing key words for your topic that you'll use to search for sources. This helps you focus your efforts right on your topic.

   Example:
   Key words for a research paper on Charlotte Perkins Gilman's "The Yellow Wall-Paper" might look like this:

   Gilman, Charlotte Perkins (author)
   "The Yellow Wall-Paper" (title)
   Mental illness (a topic in the story)
   Nineteenth-century medicine (another important topic)
   Feminism (a movement that embraced this story)

2. **Include related words.** As you list your key words, think of synonyms that you can use to expand or narrow your search.

Example:

If the topic of your research paper is overcrowding in national parks, you might include some of these synonyms:

Environmentalism
Wilderness
National monuments
Conservation
Federal lands
Government lands

Each helps you locate useful source materials.

Can't think of any synonyms or related terms for your research topic? Check the *Library of Congress Guide to Subject Headings*. This set of reference books identifies the subject headings used by the Library of Congress. It can help you find key words as well as related terms.

3. **Learn the lingo.** Nearly every research tool has an abbreviation—or two!

Examples:

The Dictionary of Library Biography is abbreviated as *DLB*.
Something About the Author is called *SATA*.

You can learn the abbreviations for print sources by checking the introduction or index. For on-line sources, check the Help screen.

4. **Know your library.** All libraries offer some special services. Many libraries get books, newspapers, and magazines for you through interlibrary loans. While libraries rarely charge for these services, they take time—often as long as two to four weeks. See your reference librarians when you start researching so that you know which special services are available, their cost (if any), and the time involved.

5. **Consult reference librarians.** After reading this guidebook, you should be able to locate nearly every ref-

erence source you need on your own. Once in a while, however, you might get stumped. Maybe you're tired; perhaps you're in an unfamiliar library.

Whatever the reason, when you have a research question that you can't answer on your own, turn to the reference librarians. They are the experts on research methods and their job is to help you find what you need. In addition, they are very well educated. Most librarians in colleges and universities, for example, are required to have earned two master's degrees, one in Information Retrieval Methods (Library Science) and one in a subject area (such as English, history, math, and so on).

Checklist of Sources

The following list summarizes the sources available. Skim it now. As you research, return to the list to help you use a range of sources.

_____ Almanacs

_____ Archival materials (rare books, charts, maps, etc.)

_____ Atlases

_____ Audio-visual materials

_____ Books

_____ Encyclopedias

_____ Essays

_____ Government documents

_____ Indexes

_____ Interviews

_____ Magazines

_____ On-line sources

_____ Pamphlets

_____ Primary sources (letters, diaries, etc.)

_____ Reviews of books, movies, plays, and TV shows

_____ Surveys

_____ Yearbooks

Chapter 6

How Do I Use Books for My Research Paper?

Be sure you go to the author to get at his meaning, not to find yours.

John Ruskin

For many students, books are an indispensable part of research. For starters, books are "user-friendly"; it's easy to open a book and start reading. You don't need any special equipment such as a computer terminal to read a book, either. Since it takes time to write and publish books, they tend to be reliable sources, but more on that in Chapter 12. Right now, you'll learn how to find the books you need to complete your research.

Classification of Books

The books you use for research papers fall into two main categories: fiction and nonfiction.

- *Fiction works* (novels and short stories) are cataloged under the author's last name.

- *Nonfiction books,* such as biographies, histories, and textbooks, are classified in two different ways: (1) by the Dewey Decimal system and (2) by the Library of Congress classification system.

You almost always use more nonfiction books than fiction books for your research. It's not unusual for a major university library to have over a million books. Even a small community library often has over 100,000 volumes.

How can you find the books you need? Librarians use call numbers and classification systems. Knowing how these systems work can help you find the books you need to complete your research.

CALL NUMBERS

Each book in the library is marked with a *call number,* which tells where the book is located in the library's stacks.

- If you are working in a library with *open stacks* (where you can roam the book collection yourself), you can copy down the call number and get the book yourself.

- If you are working in a library with *closed stacks* (the stacks are restricted to library personnel), you must fill out a call slip, hand it in at the call desk, and wait for someone to retrieve the book for you.

Some libraries have a mix of open and closed stacks.

Whether the stacks are open or closed, be sure to copy down the call number *exactly* as it appears in the card catalog. Otherwise, it is very hard—if not impossible—for you to find the book. Don't try to remember all the digits in the number as you rush to the stacks. Jot it down. Most libraries even keep small pencils and scraps of paper next to the card catalog for this purpose.

BOOK CLASSIFICATION SYSTEMS

Libraries classify their books according to one of two systems: the Dewey Decimal classification system or the Library of Congress classification system. The systems use completely different sets of letters and numbers, as you'll learn.

Dewey Decimal Classification System

Melvil Dewey (1851–1931) was a man with an obsession for order. This might have made life difficult for his family, but it revolutionized libraries. Before Dewey's system of classifying books was adopted, many libraries relied on systems that filed books by color or size. While working as a librarian at Amherst College, Dewey developed a system that is used by most elementary schools, high schools, and small public libraries today. His classification system, published in 1876, divided nonfiction books into ten broad categories, as follows:

000–099	General works such as encyclopedias
100–199	Philosophy
200–299	Religion (including mythology)
300–399	Social sciences (including folklore, legends, government, manners, vocations)
400–499	Language (including dictionaries and grammar books)
500–599	Pure science (mathematics, astronomy, chemistry, nature study)
600–699	Technology (applied science, aviation, building, engineering, homemaking)
700–799	Arts (photography, drawing, painting, music, sports)
800–899	Literature (plays, poetry)
900–999	History (ancient, modern, geography, travel)

Each of these categories is further divided for accuracy of classification.

Example:

500–599 covers pure science, such as chemistry, astronomy, mathematics, and physics.

Books on mathematics can be found from 510 to 519.

Geometry is listed under 513.

These categories are further subdivided by decimals to provide additional categories. Additional digits can be added to create even more precise categories.

Books are arranged alphabetically within each classification by the first letter of the author's last name. Therefore, a library that has several books on computer technology files them all under the same call number but shelves them alphabetically.

Library of Congress Classification System

The Dewey Decimal System was designed to suit all libraries; the Library of Congress system was created to suit one specific library, the Library of Congress. However, this classification system proved so useful that it is now used by nearly all large libraries, especially those in colleges and universities.

Each Library of Congress classification number contains three lines:

- A letter at the top.
- A number in the middle.
- A letter/number combination at the bottom.

The Library of Congress classification system has 20 classes:

A   General works
B   Philosophy and religion
C   History
D   History and topography (except America)
E-F American history
G   Geography, anthropology, folklore, manners, customs, recreation
H   Social sciences
J   Political sciences
K   United States law
L   Education
M   Music
N   Fine arts
P   Language and literature
Q   Science
R   Medicine

S   Agriculture

T   Technology

U   Military science

V   Naval science

Z   Bibliography and library science

As with the Dewey system, each of the categories in the Library of Congress system can be divided into subclasses. Because the Library of Congress system groups related topics, you can often find unexpected but related avenues to pursue as you research. As a result, it's not a bad idea to take a few minutes to browse the shelves as you gather books you need.

Warning!

Unfortunately, library call numbers don't work like the Celsius and Fahrenheit temperature systems. There is no way to convert the call numbers in one system to those in the other system. So you cannot take the call numbers from a library that uses the Dewey classification system to a library that uses the Library of Congress classification system. You have to look the book up again if you work with two systems; so it's usually a good idea to pick one library system for books—either the public library system or the university/college library system. Of course, within either system, you can use as many different libraries as you wish.

Types of Card Catalogs

A *catalog* is a detailed list of all the books in the library. There are two main types of card catalogs: print card catalogs and on-line card catalogs. Years ago, all libraries had *print card catalogs*, rows of cards in wooden boxes. You had to search through the drawers of cards by hand.

Increasingly, however, libraries have moved to *on-line catalogs*, which you access from computer terminals. These have many advantages.

Odds are good that on-line catalogs will completely replace the traditional card catalogs in the near future.

On-line catalogs are surprisingly easy to use. They have clear directions printed across the top or bottom of the screen. There's often a pull-down menu as well, which makes it even easier to see your options. If you have difficulty, ask the reference librarian.

How to Find the Books You Need

Whether you use an on-line or a paper card catalog, you can locate material in books three different ways:

- Subject search
- Title search
- Author search

Your topic determines how you search for a book. Since most research papers deal with topics and issues, you'll likely be searching by subject. However, you often have to look under titles and authors as well. Consider all three avenues of finding information as you look through the card catalog.

Reading a Catalog Entry

Knowing how to read a card catalog entry can help you gather useful information.

Example:
Here's a typical entry with explanations:

[Author]	McClanahan, Ezra
[Title]	Guide to American Art Museums
[Possible subject card headings]	1. Art--United States--Guide books
	2. Art museums--US--guidebooks
	3. Museums--US--guidebooks
[Library of Congress number]	N510.M34 1983 708.13 (Dewey Decimal No.)
	ISBN 0-564-2357630-14

Useful Books to Consider

In addition to specific books on your topic, here are some general reference sources to consider:

1. ***Encyclopedias.*** Some teachers do not let their students cite encyclopedias in their bibliographies, but that's no reason not to use them for background information. An encyclopedia can be an excellent way to get a quick, authoritative overview of your topic. This can often help you get a handle on the issues.

   There are general encyclopedias (*World Books, Britannica, Colliers, Funk and Wagnalls*) as well as technical ones. The encyclopedias can be in print or on CD-ROM. The CD-ROM form often has splashly multimedia features, such as video and sound. They tend to have less text, however; so for serious research, print encyclopedias are usually a better bet.

2. ***Books in Print.*** This is an annual listing of books currently in print or slated for print by January 31 of the following year. *Books in Print* is a multivolume set shelved in the reference section of the library. It is also available on CD-Rom.

   Why use it? *Books in Print* can tell you if a book is still being issued by the publisher. This means the library can order a copy of the book or you can buy one yourself at a book store. If the book is no longer in print, the library can get one only if it already owns it or another library has a copy.

3. ***Guide to Reference Books.*** Published by the American Library Association, this useful guide has five main categories: general reference works; humanities; social and behavioral sciences; history and area studies; and science, technology, and medicine.

4. ***Who's Who in America.*** This reference work includes biographical entries on approximately 75,000 Americans and others linked to America. *Who Was Who* covers famous people who have died.

5. **Almanacs.** These are remarkably handy and easy-to-use reference guides. These one-volume books are a great source for statistics and facts. The *World Almanac* and the *Information, Please Almanac* are the two best known almanacs. They are updated every year.

This chapter covered how you can use books as you research information. In the following chapter, you'll learn all about the many other sources that are available. These offer equally exciting research opportunities.

Chapter 7

What Other Sources Can I Use for My Research Paper?

*Research is the ability to investigate systematically
and truly all that comes under your observation in life.*

Marcus Aurelius

As you learned in Chapter 6, books are often an excellent source of material for your research paper. However, books have a number of important drawbacks when it comes to research:

- They may not be timely. Since it can take more than a year to write, edit, and publish a book, the information it contains may be out of date by the time the book appears on the library shelf. This is especially true in fast-changing areas such as medical issues and current events.

- Books are so costly that some libraries are cutting back on their purchases, putting their funds instead into on-line sources. As a result, you may not be able to get the books you need easily.

- It can take a long time to sift through a book to find the information you need. You may have to do a lot of reading to find the nugget you need.

- Books are cumbersome and heavy.

Therefore, in addition to books, you're probably going to use articles from magazines, newspapers, and journals to find information for your research paper. In some cases, you'll use far more articles than books. In this chapter, you'll learn how to find magazines, newspapers, and journals as well as interviews, media, and audio-visual sources.

Periodicals

Periodicals include all material that is published on a regular schedule—weekly, biweekly, monthly, bimonthly, four times a year, and so on. Newspapers, magazines, and journals are classified as periodicals.

PRINT INDEXES

Traditionally, every periodical was indexed in one or more print indexes. To find the magazines you needed, you looked in the appropriate print index.

Example:
To find an article in a "popular" magazine such as *Time, Mademoiselle, Atlantic, Sports Illustrated,* or *Road and Track,* look in the *Reader's Guide to Periodical Literature.* This guide, with its distinctive green cover, indexes over 100 "popular" magazines.

Follow the same procedure if you want to find newspaper articles: Check a newspaper index, such as *The New York Times Index,* a thick red book. The same is true for scholarly articles. Since print indexes are usually issued annually, they list the publications for a single year. To investigate what has been published over a number of years, you have to search several volumes.

A periodical index does not give you the actual article. Instead, it lists the *issue* of the periodical that contains the article. To get the actual article, you have to jot down the bibliographic citation, ask a clerk to retrieve the magazine, and then read it. If the magazine is on microfilm or microfiche, you have to place it in a reader and, if you wish, make a photocopy of it. Increasingly many magazines are available on-line. This makes retrieval even easier.

COMPUTERIZED DATABASES

Increasingly, libraries have been using *computerized databases* in place of print indexes. A computerized database is a bibliographic computer file of reference sources. Some databases include only periodicals; others include books, media, and even telephone numbers! No matter what information is indexed, each entry provides the title, author, and sometimes a summary.

The computer often prints the citation for you. In some cases, you can get the computer to download the entire article for you. This is the so-called *full-text* feature.

Every library has different periodical databases. Here are some of the ones you are likely to find:

- *DataTimes* is an on-line index to local newspapers.
- *DIALOG* is an extensive, well regarded database.
- *InfoTrak* lists more than 1,000 business, technological, and general-interest periodicals, as well as *The New York Times* and *The Wall Street Journal.* Many are full-text.
- *LEXIS/NEXIS* affords access to thousands of full-text articles.
- *MILCS* is a database of all the holdings of academic and public libraries in specific regions.
- *OCLC First Search* lists all the periodicals, media, and books in the United States and Canada. It has many indexes.
- *VU/TEXT* is a newspaper database.
- *WILSONSEARCH* is an on-line information system containing the Wilson databases not on CD-ROM.

Example:
It contains the *Education Index and the Index to Legal Periodicals.*

In addition, many libraries carry their periodical indexes on CD-ROM. CD-ROM indexes usually cover several years of publication, making them more comprehensive than a single print volume of an index.

- WILSONDISC, for example, is a series of six databases on CD-ROM that you can easily search on your own. The six databases are:

  Applied Science and Technology Index.

  Business Periodicals Index.

  General Science Index.

  Humanities Index.

  Reader's Guide to Periodical Literature.

  Social Science Index.
- ERIC is an education index on CD-ROM. It can search for articles and books by subject or keyword.

You use the same search strategy with on-line and CD-ROM databases as you do with a print index: Use key words, title, author, or any combination of these.

Be Complete

While more and more libraries are replacing their print indexes with on-line and CD-ROM sources, many libraries still maintain their print indexes. In addition, the CD-ROM or on-line databases may not go back far enough for the sources you need. This is especially true if you are doing historical or literary research. As a result, to do a complete search for materials, you must use everything that pertains to your topic. This often means using both print and on-line indexes.

Warning!

Be sure the index you're searching lists the kind of sources you want. Otherwise, it might appear that library doesn't have any material on your topic if you're in the wrong index.

Example:

In the Humanities Index you would probably not find any articles on stock mutual funds. For this topic, you should check the Business Index.

Interviews and Surveys

Although you'll probably conduct most of your research in the library, remember that you can find a great deal of material in laboratories, in courthouses, and in private archives. Consider the possibility of conducting original research for your own paper. You can do this by interviewing knowledgeable people and by devising and distributing questionnaires.

INTERVIEWS

Interviews allow you to conduct primary research and acquire valuable information unavailable in print and on-line sources. By including quotations from people who have direct knowledge of a subject, you add considerable authority and immediacy to your paper. You can conduct interviews by telephone, by e-mail, or in person.

Whom should you interview? Include only *respected people* in the field, such as noted experts, recognized authorities, and credentialed professionals. Don't waste your time with cranks and people with private agendas.

Also:

- Call and confirm the interview.
- Prepare a series of questions well in advance of the interview. The questions should all focus on your topic and the person's recognized area of expertise.
- After the interview, write a note thanking the person for his or her time.
- Get the person's permission *beforehand* if you decide to tape-record the interview.
- Obtain a signed release for the right to use their remarks on the record.

SURVEYS

Surveys are useful when you want to measure the behavior or attitudes of a fairly large group. On the basis of the responses, you can draw some conclusions. Such generalizations are usually made in quantitative terms.

Example:
Fewer than one-third of the respondents said that they favored further governmental funding for schools.

If you decide to create a survey, follow these guidelines:

- Be sure to get a large enough *sampling* to make your results fair and unbiased. Include at least fifty people, but this is one instance where more *is* better!
- Don't ask loaded questions that lead people toward a specific response. Be sure your questions are neutral and unbiased.
- To get honest answers to your questions, it is essential to guarantee your respondents' anonymity. Written surveys are best for this purpose.
- Make the form simple and easy. Few people are willing to take the time to fill out a long, complex form.
- Carefully tabulate your results. Check your math.

In addition, many topics have been extensively discussed by experts on respected television news programs and documentaries. It is often possible to write to the television station and obtain printed transcripts of the programs. You might also be able to videotape the programs or borrow copies of the programs that have already been recorded.

Audiovisual Sources

In addition, you may be able to use audiovisual sources for your research paper. These include:

- Records.
- Audio cassettes.
- Video tapes.
- Slides.
- Photographs.

You can often borrow audiovisual materials from your library as you would books, magazines, and other print sources.

Other Sources of Information

You're not done yet! The library has even more sources for you to consider. These include government documents, pamphlets, and special collections.

GOVERNMENT DOCUMENTS

Who's the largest publisher in the United States? It's the federal government! The government publishes numerous pamphlets, reports, catalogs, and newsletters on most issues of national concern. Government documents are often excellent research sources because they tend to be factual and unbiased. To find government documents, try these CD-ROM and on-line indexes:

- *Monthly Catalogue of the United States Government Publications*
- *United States Government Publications Index*

Many government offices have extensive on-line sites where you can download an astonishing treasure of information, including the full text of many documents and research papers. Some of these sites are listed in the almanac; others are available through search engines and key words.

PAMPHLETS

Pamphlets published by private organizations and government agencies are another reference source. Since pamphlets are usually too small to place on the shelves, they are stored in the *vertical file*. This is just what the name implies: a filing cabinet with pamphlets arranged in files. *The Vertical File Index: A Subject and Title Index to Selected Pamphlet Material* lists many of the available titles. In addition, you can simply browse in the vertical file under your topic.

SPECIAL COLLECTIONS

Many libraries also have special collections of rare books, manuscripts, newspapers, magazines, photographs, maps, and items of local interest. These are stored in a special room or section of the library. Often you need permission to access these materials.

This chapter covered all the nonbook reference materials available: periodicals, interviews, surveys, audiovisual information, government documents, pamphlets, and special collections. Chapter 8 teaches you how to use electronic media. You're going to really enjoy this!

How Do I Use Electronic Media?

You should always collect more material than you will eventually use.

WILLIAM ZINSSER

The Internet contains lists of sources and the sources themselves, which you can read on screen or transfer to your own computer. Read on to find out more about this useful reference source.

What Is the Internet?

The *Internet* is an expanding global information computer network. It's made of people, hardware (computers), and software (computer programs). Each regional network is linked to other regional networks around the world to create a network of networks: the Internet. It's rapidly changing the way we gather information and communicate.

With the proper equipment, you can access information from around the world—including text, graphics, sound, and video. From your computer, you can view masterpieces from the Louvre Museum in France, take an aerial tour of Hawaii, or dissect a virtual frog. You can search databases at the Library of Congress and read electronic newsletters. This makes the Internet a valuable source of information as you prepare your research papers.

World Wide Web

The *World Wide Web* (www) is a network of pathways through the Internet that connects "pages" of material—whatever can be sent electronically.

The World Wide Web is made of documents called *Web pages,* which can combine text, pictures, and sound. The *home page* is the entry point for access to a collection of pages. Specific words, pictures, or *icons* (special places to click) act as links to other pages. It doesn't matter where the other pages are located. Even if they are on the other side of the world, the computer programs retrieve them automatically for you.

Searching the Web

The Web is not like a library where information has been arranged within an accepted set of rules. It's more like a garage sale, where items of similar nature are usually grouped together—but not always. As a result, you'll find treasures side by side with trash. And, like a garage sale, the method of organization on the Web shifts constantly.

So how can you search the Web for information to use in your research paper? There are several different ways, each of them surprisingly easy. Here's how they work.

SEARCH ENGINES

Search engines, which work with *keywords,* help you locate Web sites. You type in a keyword, and the search engine automatically looks through its giant databases for matches.

The more narrow the phrase, the better your chances for finding the precise information you need.

Example:
If you're interested in a college, don't use "college" as a keyword. You'll get millions and millions of responses. Instead, name a specific

college, such as "The State University of New York at Farmingdale." This gets you to the precise Web page you need.

Here are some of the most popular search engines.

- **AltaVista.** It processes more than 2.5 million search requests a day. It's at http://www.altavista.digital.com.

- **Excite.** It has a database of 1.5 million Web pages that you can search by keyword or concept. It's at http://www.excite.com.

- **HotBot.** You can search by file name, geographic location, domain, and Web site. It's at http://www.hot-box.com.

- **InfoSeek.** This is a full-text search system. It's at http://www2.infoseek.com.

- **Yahoo.** One of the most famous search engines, Yahoo lists more than 200,000 Web sites in more than 20,000 categories. You can access other search engines from Yahoo as well. It's at http://www.yahoo.com.

- **WebCrawler.** It is used by America Online and can be found at http://webcrawler.com.

Since not all search engines lead to the same sources, you should use more than one. *Bookmarks* or *hot lists* (accompanying each search engine) help you mark sources to which you want to return.

URLS

If you already have the address for a Web site, the *URL* (*Uniform Resource Locator*), you can type it in. URLs are made of long strings of letters.

Example:

The address for the World Wide Web Virtual Library subject catalog is:

http://www.w3.org/pub./DataSources/bySubject/Overview.html

It's crucial that you type the address *exactly* as it appears. Pay special attention to periods, capital letters, and lower-case letters. If you are off so much as a capital letter, you won't reach the site. So if you're not getting anywhere with your search, check your typing for spelling and accuracy.

WAIS

Pronounced "ways" and standing for *Wide Area Information Service,* WAIS enables you to search for key words in the actual text of documents. This increases the likelihood that a document you've identified has information on your topic. You can use WAIS to search Web documents. See a reference librarian for detailed instructions.

NEWS GROUPS

News groups are comprised of people interested in a specific topic who share information electronically. You can communicate with them through:

- A *Listserv,* an electronic mailing list for subscribers interested in a specific topic.
- Or *Usenet,* special-interest news groups open to the public.

Your reference librarian can help you hop aboard.

These sources allow you to keep up with the most recent developments in your area of research and may also point you to useful information and resources that could have taken you a long time to find on your own.

E-MAIL

E-mail (electronic mail) lets you communicate electronically with specific people. Senders and receivers must have e-mail addresses. Specific programs act as "phone books" to help you find the person you are looking for.

Example:
Try locating someone through www.people.yahoo.com.

No matter how you search the Internet, there is help available electronically. Look for introductory screens, welcome messages, or files with names like "?", "Readme," "About...," "FAQ" (Frequently Asked Questions), or "Formulating a search with... ."

Great Places

The following list contains some useful places to visit on the Web as you begin your research.

Note:
Every care has been taken to make this list timely and correct. But just as people move, so do Web sites. Since this book was published, the Web site may have moved. In that case, look for a forward link. If not, use "keyword" to find the new site.

1. Guide to the Web
   http://www.hcc.hawaii.edu/guide/www.guide.html
2. Internet Resources
   http://www.ncsa.uiuc.edu/SDG/Software/Mosaic/Meta Index.html
3. Library of Congress
   http://www.lcweb.loc.gov
4. List of Web Servers
   http://www.info.cern.ch/hypertext/DataSources/WWW/ Servers.html
5. Newspaper Links
   http://www.spub.ksu.edu/other/journal.html
6. Sports
   http://www.atm.ch.cam.ac.uk/sports/sports.html
7. U.S. Federal Agencies
   http://www.lib.lsu.edu/gov/fedgov.html
   http://www.fedworld.gov
8. Who's Who on the Internet
   http://www.web.city.ac.ik/citylive/pages.html
9. Nova-Links
   http://www.nova.edu/Inter-Links
10. Virtual Tourist World Map
    http://www.wings.buffalo.edu/world

Hints for Searching on the Internet

The Internet presents a vast number of widely distributed resources covering thousands of topics and providing many options for research in many fields. Often there is so much information that you may not know where to begin. Or maybe you haven't been able to locate what you're seeking.

THE INTERNET IS EVER-CHANGING

When people search on the Internet for a particular topic, they automatically let their past research experiences take over. As a result, many students start searching for library catalogs and reference materials.

These approaches may not always work because everything on the Internet is constantly being updated, improved, relocated, shuffled, and cut. When you do your search, don't expect something that you found today to be there tomorrow—or even a hour later. If you find material and need it, keep a copy of it. It's not enough to write down the address and plan on locating the site later.

BOOLEAN SEARCH

One of the best strategies to find a subject on the Internet is to use a *Boolean search*. It uses the terms "and," "or," and "not" to expand or restrict a search. Here's how they work:

And   If you link two terms with "and" you get all the works containing both terms.

> **Example:**
> If you tell an electronic search tool to look for "national parks" and "pollution" alone, it lists all the works having to do with either subject. But if you link them with the word "and" by typing in "national parks and pollution," the computer narrows your search to only those sources in which both terms appear.

Or   If you link two terms with "or," the search leads to all sources that contain *either* term.

Example:
Linking "national parks" with "pollution" tells the computer to list only works with *either* term.

Not Using "not" narrows a search.

Example:
Telling the search engine to look for "national parks not Bryce Canyon" leads to all sources about national parks *except* those mentioning Bryce Canyon.

Relax!

No one is an expert on every facet of the Internet—it's simply impossible. While many people are skilled with the tools and have a good idea where to look for information on many topics, no one can keep up with the information flow. Fortunately, you don't have to understand everything to use the Internet quickly and easily. All you need are a computer, modem, and the time to explore different paths.

This chapter helped you hop aboard the Information Superhighway and start using electronic sources for research. Chapter 9 shows you how to track your research.

How Do I Track My Research?

*Research means to give each and every element
its final value by grouping it in the unity of
an organized whole.*

PIERRE T. DECHARDIN

As you start to gather your information, you'll need a systematic way to organize it. What you want is an organized list of sources, a *bibliography*. You'll use this list to locate sources and, as you write your research paper, to document the information you used. In this chapter, you'll learn how to make a working bibliography.

Making Bibliography Cards

As you find each source on your topic, record the publication and location information. When you first start researching, you may just print this information from electronic sources and indexes. Later, you'll turn it into bibliography cards written in the appropriate format.

To do so, get a pack of 3×5 index cards. Use one card per source. These are your *bibliography cards*. Cards allow you to keep the most promising sources and discard the irrelevant ones at your convenience. Also, cards can easily be arranged in alphabetical order when the time comes to type a "Works Cited" page for inclusion at the end of your paper.

There are several different *bibliographic styles,* that is, ways of documenting sources. As you write your bibliography cards, follow the documenting style assigned by your instructor or preferred by the discipline in which you are writing.

- Use the *Modern Language Association (MLA)* style for research papers in the humanities, including literature, history, the arts, and religion.

- Use the *American Psychological Association (APA)* style for research papers in the social sciences, such as psychology and sociology.

For sample MLA citations, see Chapter 17.

TRADITIONAL BIBLIOGRAPHY CARDS

What should you include on your bibliography cards? Here are some models.

Books

On the bibliography card, note anything you are going to need to retrieve the book. Relevant information includes:

- Call number.
- Author/editor.
- Title.
- Place of publication.
- Publisher.
- Date.
- Library where you found the book.

This last detail is very important, since it can save you a great deal of time and effort if you are using more than one library.

Example:

Call number

Author/editor

```
PR
2981.
M77
Muir, Kenneth, ed. Shakespeare:
The Comedies. Englewood Cliffs,
New Jersey: Prentice-Hall, Inc.,
1998.
                         publisher
date
Location: Farmingdale Library
```

Title
Place of publication

Location of source

Periodicals

On the bibliography card, include:

- Author.
- Title of the article.
- Title of the periodical.
- Date of the article.
- Volume number.
- Page numbers.
- Library.

You may also want to note if the article contained pictures or illustrations that you may wish to consult.

Example:

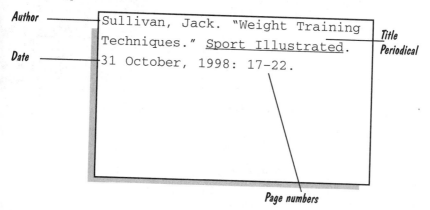

Author

Date

```
Sullivan, Jack. "Weight Training
Techniques." Sport Illustrated.
31 October, 1998: 17-22.
```

Title
Periodical

Page numbers

Electronic Sources

On your card, note:

- Medium (e.g., CD-ROM, on-line).
- Computer service.
- Date of your search.
- URL (electronic address).

Example:

On-line Web site

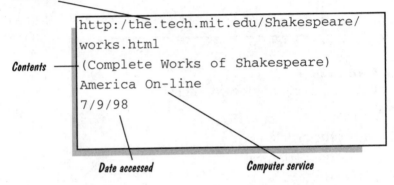

Contents

```
http:/the.tech.mit.edu/Shakespeare/
works.html
(Complete Works of Shakespeare)
America On-line
7/9/98
```

Date accessed   *Computer service*

Interviews

On these cards, include:

- Name of the person interviewed.
- Person's area of expertise.
- Person's address and telephone.
- Date of the interview.

Example:

Subject

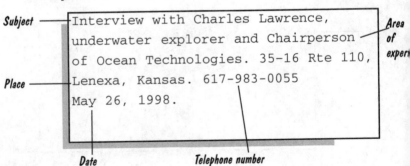

Place

```
Interview with Charles Lawrence,
underwater explorer and Chairperson
of Ocean Technologies. 35-16 Rte 110,
Lenexa, Kansas. 617-983-0055
May 26, 1998.
```

Area of expert

Date   *Telephone number*

Warning!

If a catalog or index does not provide complete bibliographic information, leave blanks to be filled in later when you have the actual source.

COMPUTERIZED "BIBLIOGRAPHY CARDS"

Some people prefer to make their "bibliography cards" on a computer. This method has several advantages. First, you can update, alphabetize, and correct your cards as you go along. Second, at the end of the project, you can rework this file to convert it to your Works Cited list of sources.

However, be sure to back up your "cards" on floppy disks. In addition, print out hard copies as you work. This way, you won't lose your material if your hard drive crashes or the file develops a glitch.

Developing a Working Bibliography

When you start your research, your teacher may ask you to prepare a *working bibliography* listing the sources you plan to use. Your working bibliography differs from your Works Cited page in its scope: Your working bibliography is much larger. Your Works Cited page includes only those sources you actually cite in your paper.

To prepare a working bibliography, arrange your bibliography cards in the order required by your documentation system (MLA, ALA, etc.), and copy the entries on a sheet of paper following the correct form.

Developing an Annotated Bibliography

Some instructors may ask you to create an *annotated bibliography* as a middle step between your working bibliography and your Works Cited page. An annotated bibliography is the same as a working bibliography except it includes comments about the sources. These notes enable your teacher to assess your progress.

Example:
You might note that some sources are difficult to find, hard to read, or especially useful.

This chapter explained how to make useful bibliography cards so that you can track your research painlessly. In Chapter 10, you'll find out how to evaluate your sources—and why it's crucial that you do so.

How Do I Evaluate Sources?

*Nobody outside a baby carriage or a judge's chambers
believes in an unprejudiced point of view.*

LILLIAN HELLMAN

"All the news that fits we print" might be the unofficial
motto of a free press. One of the great strengths of a free
press is its ability to print anything that does not libel its
subject. As far as researchers are concerned, however, that
very freedom presents its own problems. *A source that appears
in print, in the media, or on-line is not necessarily valid.* As a
result, you must carefully evaluate every source you find
before you use it. This means that you must read critically
and carefully.

As you gather your sources, evaluate them carefully.
Here are the three main criteria to use as you determine
whether a source is valid for inclusion in your research
paper:

1. Quality
2. Bias
3. Appropriateness

Let's look at each criterion in detail.

Quality

As Spencer Tracey said about Katharine Hepburn in the movie *Adam's Rib,* "There's not much meat on her, but what there is is choice."

The same is true for movie stars as it is for research source materials: Quality counts. You want only the choice cuts for your research paper. If the material isn't of the highest quality, it won't support your thesis, convince your readers of your point, or stand up under your reader's scrutiny. In fact, it will have just the opposite effect. That's why it's important to evaluate the quality of every source before you decide to include it in your research paper.

The old maxim is true: You *can't* judge a book by its cover. You have to go deeper. Here's how to do it:

- **Check the writer's qualifications.** Is the writer or speaker *really* qualified to write on the subject? Is this someone you trust for a valid opinion? You can use the following simple checklist to evaluate the writer or speaker:

  _____ Is the person an expert or an eyewitness to the events described in the source?

  _____ What is the person's reputation?

  Example:
  You can check in biographical source books such as *Contemporary Biography, Who's Who,* and *Who Was Who* to validate a person's reputation. Anthologies often contain biographical information about the various contributors, too.

  _____ Does the person have the credentials to write on this subject?

  Example:
  Don't be fooled by degrees. A Ph.D. in chemistry doesn't give a scholar the credentials to write about biology, physics, or any other subject outside his or her field.

  _____ Is the author well known and respected in the field? How many other books or articles has the author published on the subject?

_____ Does the author have a bias or a personal agenda to advance? Check the author's credentials and reputation to see if you can discern bias; pay attention to **tone** as well.

- **Evaluate the source itself.** Here are some guidelines to use:

_____ Was the source well reviewed?

Read some critical reviews in quality journals and newspapers to find out how the experts evaluated the book. If the book was not reviewed, it may not be on the front line of scholarship.

_____ Who spoke in favor of the book?

Most books have endorsements (called "blurbs") penned by well known people in the field. These usually appear on the back cover of the dust jacket. See whether the endorsements were written by respected writers, scholars, and public figures. If not, the book may not be a solid source. A reliable blurb is not the final word, however; so be sure to verify completely, as described here.

_____ Is the publisher reputable? Is it known for publishing reliable information?

Reputable sources include scholarly journals, university presses, and major publishers.

_____ Is the source up-to-date? What is the publication date?

_____ Is the source a first edition, revision, or reprint?

While the information in first editions is usually up-to-date, the book may be so new that it has not yet had time to be authenticated and replicated.

_____ Is the source complete? Have certain facts been cut for their controversial nature or for space limitations? To make sure a source is complete, check it in more than one version—especially if it's a crucial source.

_____ Does the author present sufficient evidence to support the thesis?

_____ Does the author document his or her claims with the titles and authors of source materials? Are these sources credible?

_____ Can the claims in the source be backed up in other sources?

Be especially suspicious of sources that claim to have the "secret" or "inside track." If you can't find the same information in other sources, the material doesn't hold up to scrutiny.

_____ Is the source fair, or does it contain distorted information? The following section shows you how to evaluate sources for bias.

Bias

Every source is biased, because every source has a point of view. Bias is not necessarily bad, as long as you recognize it as such and take it into account as you evaluate and use the source.

Example:
An article on hunting published in *Field and Stream* is likely to have a very different slant from an article on the same subject published in *Vegetarian Times*.

Problems arise when the bias isn't recognized or acknowledged. Here are some problem areas to watch:

1. **Bogus claims.** A claim can be considered *bogus*, or false, when the speaker promises more than he or she can deliver.

Example:
The speaker may speak vaguely of "many important experiments" or "recent clinical studies" to prove a point. The point may indeed

have value, but the studies the speaker cites as proof are too fuzzy to have merit.

Well educated people are rightly skeptical about promises from strangers.

Effective research sources use specific support, not just vague references to unidentified studies and sources. You can't evaluate "many important experiments" or "recent clinical studies" unless you know how they were undertaken, by whom, and where the results were published.

Also be on the lookout for sources that refer to "statistics that show... ." Statistics can be very useful in proving a point, but they can also be misleading—especially if you don't have the numbers to evaluate their validity. Ask yourself:

- Do the statistics raise any unanswered questions?
- Has the source of the statistics been revealed?

"Well known" information is another form of bogus claim. Be wary of sources that tell you that "Everybody knows that..." or "It is a well known fact that ... ." If the fact is so "well known," why is the writer bothering to cite it as support? Very likely, it's the best support the writer can muster—which doesn't speak well for the validity of the source or writer.

2. **Loaded terms.** Suspect sources may use "loaded terms" to make their point. A term becomes *loaded* when it is asked to carry more emotional weight than its context can legitimately support. As a result, it becomes *slanted* or *biased*. These sources are often not reliable.

Words with strong *connotations* (emotional responses) often show bias.

Example:
A writer refers to the governor's "regime" rather than "administration." "Regime" is a loaded term because it is used to describe oppressive military dictatorships.

While loaded terms are most often used in political writing and speech, they can appear in any source. That's why it's important to read critically.

3. **Misrepresentation.** This type of bias takes many forms. First, a writer or speaker can lie outright. Or a writer may be more subtle, inventing false data or "facts." In addition, dishonest writers often twist what their opponents have said. To misrepresent people this way, they use oversimplification. A complex argument can be reduced to ridicule in a slogan, or an important element of an argument can be skipped over.

How can you protect yourself from being misled by this type of bias? Here are some issues to consider as you evaluate a text for misrepresentation:

- Is someone quoted out of context?
- Are facts or statistics cited in a vacuum?
- Does the quotation reflect the overall content of the source or does it merely reflect a minor detail?
- Has key information been omitted?

To verify this, be sure to check two versions of the source. Remember, if something looks too good to be true, it probably is!

Appropriateness

Even if a source passes the first two tests and proves to be of high quality and free from bias, it may still not belong in your research paper. For a source to make the final cut, it has to fit with your audience, purpose, and tone. It must be *appropriate* to your paper. How can you decide if a source is suitable for inclusion in your research paper? Try these suggestions:

- Do you understand the material in the source?
- If the source is too technical for you to grasp fully, you might not use it correctly in your paper.
- Is the source written at a level appropriate to your readers?
- Does this source have the information you need?
- Does the source suit your purposes in this research paper?

A Special Note on Evaluating Electronic Sources

Be especially leery of electronic sources that you'll find on the Internet. They can be difficult to authenticate and validate. Unlike most print resources such as magazines and journals that go through a filtering process (e.g., editing, peer review), information on the Web is mostly unfiltered. What does this mean for you? Using and citing information found over the Web is a little like swimming on a beach without a lifeguard.

PORTABLE VS. ON-LINE SOURCES

As a result, you have to use electronic sources with special care. To evaluate electronic sources, first see if the source is portable or on-line.

- *Portable sources,* such as CD-ROMs and encyclopedias, are like printed books: They have credited writers and publishers. In addition, they change only when a new version is issued. As a result, you can determine their value as you would a book.

- *On-line sources,* in contrast, may be published anonymously. This means you can't evaluate the writer or writers. Also, they can be updated and revised without notification. Further, they may vanish without warning. This makes it difficult to evaluate their reliability.

HEADER, BODY, AND FOOTER

Once you've determined that you are dealing with an on-line source, check the Web document for its three main elements: head, body and footer. Within each of these pieces, you should be able to determine the following vital elements for evaluating information:

1. **Author or contact person** (usually located in the footer)

   As you evaluate the selection, ask yourself:

   - Who is the author of the piece?

- Is the author the original creator of the information?
- Does the author list his or her occupation, years of experience, position, or education?
- With this information or lack of it, do you feel this person is qualified to write on the given topic?
- Where does the on-line source come from? Knowing the source of the site can help you evaluate its purpose and potential bias.

Example:

A business has a different slant from a university. It's likely that the business wants to sell you a product or a service, while the university is probably seeking to disseminate knowledge.

You can often find clues to the origin of an on-line source in its address (URL, or Uniform Resource Locator). Look for the suffix to identify the source. Here are the common URL suffixes you'll encounter:

Suffix	Meaning
com	Commercial (business or company)
edu	Education (academic site)
gov	Government
int	International organization
mil	Military organization
net	Internet administration
org	Other organizations, including nonprofit, nonacademic, and nongovernmental groups
sci	Special knowledge news group

2. **Link to local home page** (usually located either in header or footer) and *institution* (usually located in either header or footer). As you evaluate the selection, ask yourself:

- What institution (company, government, university, etc.) or Internet provider supports this information?

- If it is a commercial Internet provider, does the author appear to have any affiliation with a larger institution?
- If it is an institution, is it a national institution?
- Does the institution appear to filter the information appearing under its name?
- Does the author's affiliation with this particular institution appear to bias the information?

3. **Date of creation or revision** (usually located in footer).
   - When was the information created or last updated?

4. **Intended audience** (determined by examining the body).

5. **Purpose of the information**, i.e., does it inform, explain, or persuade (determined by examining the body)?

Given all the information you determined from these clues, is this piece of information appropriate for your topic? If yes, explain your decision and express any reservations as you would with any other information.

In summary, all sources are *not* equally valid. Be sure to carefully and completely evaluate every source you find before you decide whether to use it in your research paper. Weak or inaccurate sources can seriously damage your credibility as a writer and thinker.

Now that you've made sure your sources are solid, it's time to learn how to document them. It's all covered in the next chapter.

Chapter 11

How Do I Document My Sources?

One of the skills of research is knowing when you have enough information; in considering too many side issues or too many perspectives, you may lose the main thread of your subject.

CHARLES BAZERMAN

Use sources to help you advance the thesis you have defined. The sources back up your point and help you make new connections among ideas. No matter how many sources you use, their purpose remains the same: to help you make the points you want to make. That's what this chapter is all about.

Reading for Research

Now that you've gathered all your sources (or the vast majority of them), it's time to take notes on the relevant material. "Relevant" is the key word. How can you tell what you need for your paper and what should end up in the scrap heap?

In most cases you can't tell what's going to make the cut and what won't. As a result, you usually take far more notes than you need. Don't worry: Nearly all researchers wind up with extra notes. The deeper you dig into your subject, however, the more perceptive you become about what you need to prove your point most convincingly. Here are some guide-lines to help you get started:

- Before you start reading, arrange your sources according to difficulty. Read the general, introductory sources first. Use these to lay the foundation for the more specialized and technical material.

- Look for facts, expert opinions, explanations, and examples that illustrate ideas.

- Note any controversies swirling around your topic. Pay close attention to both sides of the issue: It's a great way to test the validity of your thesis.

- Read in chunks. Finish an entire paragraph, page, or chapter before you stop to take notes. This helps you get the entire picture so that you can pounce on the juicy bits of information.

Taking Notes

You can't remember all the material you read, or keep Expert A's opinion straight from Expert B's opinion. That's why you need to take notes.

For very brief research papers, you can usually gather information without taking notes. In these cases, photocopy the sources, highlight key points, jot ideas in the margins, and start drafting. But with longer, more complex research papers, you have to make note cards to handle the flow of information efficiently. Make note cards with any research paper more than a page or two long.

CARD SIZE

Many writers take notes on 4×6 index cards. This size is ideal. You don't want cards so small that you can't fit any-thing on them—or cards so large that you end up wasting most of the space.

Increasingly, however, writers have been adapting this same method to word processing technology. It's very easy to do and can save you a great deal of time when it comes to drafting. Adjust your margins to make a template for a

"Notes" file by creating 4×6-sized boxes. You can print and cut the cards as you go along. As always, when you are working on a computer, back up all your files on disks.

OVERALL GUIDELINES

Regardless of how you choose to take notes, the overall techniques remain the same. Here are the guidelines:

- Label each card with a subtopic, in the top right- or left-hand corner.

- Include a reference citation showing the source of the information. Place this in the bottom right- or left-hand corner.

- Be sure to include a page number, if the source is print.

- Write one piece of information per card.

- Keep the note short. If you write too much, you'll be right back where you started—trying to separate the essential information from the nonessential information.

- Be sure to mark direct quotes with quotation marks. This can help you avoid plagiarism later.

- Add any personal comments you think are necessary. This helps you remember how you intend to use the note in your research paper.

- Check and doublecheck your notes. Be sure you've spelled all names right and copied dates correctly. Check that you've spelled the easy words correctly, too; many errors creep in because writers overlook the obvious words.

NOTE-TAKING METHODS

There are three main ways to take notes: direct quotations, summarizing, and paraphrasing.

Taking Direct Quotations

A *direct quotation* is word for word; you copy the material exactly as it appears in the source. If there is an error in the source, you even copy that, writing [*sic*] next to the mistake. Show that a note is a direct quotation by surrounding it by quotation marks (" ").

In general, quote briefly when you take notes. Remember that long quotations are difficult to integrate into your paper. Besides, readers often find long quotations hard to follow and boring to read.

What should you quote?

- **Quote key points,** passages that sum up the main idea in a pithy way.

- **Quote subtle ideas.** Look for passages whose meaning would be watered down or lost if you summarized or paraphrased them.

- **Quote expert opinions.** They carry weight in your paper and make it persuasive.

- **Quote powerful writing.** If the passage is memorable or famous, it gives your research paper authority.

Example:

Subtopic: Nez Perce surrender

"It is cold, and we have no blankets; the little children are freezing to death. My people, some of them, have run away to the hills, and have no blankets, no food. No one knows where they are--perhaps freezing to death. I want to have time to look for my children, to see how many of them I can find. Maybe I shall find them among the dead. Hear me, my chiefs! I am tired; my heart is sick and sad. From where the sun now stands I will fight no more forever."

Comments: Very moving, emotional speech. Shows tragic consequences of displacement of Native Americans.

Lend Me Your Ears: Great Speeches in History, p. 108

Summarizing

A *summary* is a smaller version of the original, reducing the passage to its essential meaning. Be sure to summarize carefully so that you don't distort the meaning of the original passage. What should you summarize?

- Commentaries
- Explanations

86

- Evaluations
- Background information
- A writer's line of thinking or argument

Example:

Original

"Now, why am I opposed to capital punishment? It is too horrible a thing for the state to undertake. We are told by my friend, 'Oh, the killer does it; why shouldn't the state?' I would hate to live in a state that I didn't think was better than a murderer.

"But I told you the real reason. The people of a state kill a man because he killed someone else—that is all—without the slightest logic, without the slightest application to life, simply from anger, nothing else!

"I am against it because I believe it is inhuman, because I believe that as the hearts of men have softened they have gradually gotten rid of brutal punishment, because I believe it will only be a few years until it will be banished forever from every civilized country—even New York—because I believe that it has no effect whatever to stop murder."

Summary

```
Subtopic: Clarence Darrow against capital punishment

Rage and a desire for retribution are not sufficient
justification for capital punishment. It is a cruel,
inhuman, and uncivilized form of punishment. Further,
capital punishment does nothing to deter crime. For
these reasons, he believes capital punishment will soon
be eliminated, even in NY.

Comments: Original speech has an ironic, sarcastic tone.

Lend Me Your Ears: Great Speeches in History, p. 108
```

Paraphrasing

A *paraphrase* is a restatement of the writer's original words. It often includes examples and explanations from the original quotation. A paraphrase may be longer than the original, shorter than the original, or the same length.

Paraphrasing is the most difficult form of note taking. As a result, it is where beginning writers are most likely to commit *plagiarism*—using someone else's words as their own. You can avoid this by quoting words you copy directly and being very sure that you do indeed restate the material in your own words.

What should you paraphrase?

- Material that readers might otherwise misunderstand.
- Information that is important but too long to include in the original form.

Example:

Original

"In the long history of the world, only a few generations have been granted the role of defending freedom in its hour of maximum danger. I do not shrink from that responsibility—I welcome it. I do not believe that any of us would exchange places with any other people or any other generation. The energy, the faith, the devotion which we bring to this endeavor will light our country and all who serve it—and the glow from that fire can truly light the world.

"And so, my fellow Americans, ask not what your country can do for you—ask what you can do for your country."

Paraphrase

```
Topic: Social responsibility (JFK Inauguration speech)

America faces great peril. As a result, America is now
faced with the challenge of standing up for liberty. Not
many countries have ever been in this position. Kennedy
welcomes this challenge because he believes his actions
(and America's valiant response) can stand as a beacon
for the rest of the world to follow.

"And so, my fellow Americans, ask not what your country
can do for you--ask what you can do for your country."

Comments: A very famous and stirring speech.

Lend Me Your Ears: Great Speeches in History, p. 108
```

Warning!

Don't rely too heavily on any one source—no matter how good it looks. It's fairly common to find one source that seems to say it all, and just the way you like. But if you take too much from one source, you end up doing a book report, not a research paper. And, as a worst-case scenario, what happens if the source turns out to be invalid or dated? Your paper is totaled.

Now it's time to organize your research into a logical whole. Outlines are a quick and easy way to do this. Chapter 12 covers everything you wanted to know about outlines.

Part III

Drafting

How Do I Outline? (and Why?)

A foolish consistency is the hobgoblin of little minds,
Adored by statesmen and philosophers and divines.
RALPH WALDO EMERSON

As this quote indicates, the New England philosopher Ralph Waldo Emerson wasn't overly concerned with order. Where research papers are concerned, however, order is essential. And there's no better way to show the order of your ideas than with an *outline*. The purpose of an outline is to organize the material you're going to use to prove your thesis. If your information isn't arranged in a logical fashion, your reader won't be able to understand your point.

Why Create an Outline?

Some instructors require you to submit a formal outline with your research paper. These instructors understand that an outline serves as a preview tool that allows them to grasp your thesis and organization at a glance. It explains the scope and direction of your paper as well.

Even if you're not required to submit an outline, making an outline is a superb way to help you construct and classify your ideas. In addition, an outline serves as a final check that your paper is unified and coherent. It helps you see where you need to revise and edit your writing, too.

How to Create an Outline

While outlining is not difficult, it can be hard to get started. The following suggestions can make the task easier.

1. First, arrange your notes in a logical order to follow as you write. If you are having difficulty seeing an order, look for clues in the sequence of your ideas. You can make a diagram, such as a flow chart, to help you visualize the best order.
2. Jot down major headings.
3. Sort the material to fit under the headings. Revise the headings, order, or both, as necessary.
4. Look for relationships among ideas and group them as subtopics.
5. Try to avoid long lists of subtopics. Consider combining these into related ideas. In nearly all cases, your paper is better for having linked related ideas.
6. If you can't decide where to put something, put it in two or more places in the outline. As you write, you can decide which place is the most appropriate.
7. If you're not sure that an idea fits, write yourself a reminder to see where it belongs after you've written your first draft.
8. If an important idea doesn't fit, write a new outline with a place for it. If it's important, it belongs in the paper.
9. Accept your outline as a working draft. Revise and edit it as you proceed.
10. Let your outline sit a few days. Then look at it again and see what ideas don't seem to fit, which points need to be expanded, and so on. No matter how carefully you construct your outline, it will inevitably change. Don't be discouraged by these changes; they are part of the writing process.

Outline Form

Outlines are written in a specific form, observing specific rules.

General Model:

Thesis statement: Write your thesis statement here.

I. Major topics or paragraphs are indicated by Roman numerals (I, III, III). These are made by using the capital I, V, or X on your keyboard.
   A. Subheads are indicated by capital letters.
      1. Details are indicated by numbers, followed by a period.
         a. Indicate more specific details with lower-case letters.
         b. These are written a, b, c, and so forth.
      2. Begin each entry with a capital letter.
   B. You can have as many entries as you like, but there must be at least two in each category.
      1. You cannot have an I with a II.
      2. You cannot have an A without a B.
      3. You cannot have a I without a 2.
      4. You cannot have a lower-case a without a lower-case b.
II. Try to keep the entries in parallel order.
   A. There are word entries.
   B. There are phrase entries.
   C. There are sentence entries.

Note:

For examples, see the sample outlines at the end of the chapter.

Jotted Outline

A *jotted outline* is a sketch of an outline, a list of the major points you want to cover. A jotted outline is a useful way to organize your thoughts because you can see what you're including at a glance.

General Model:

Thesis: Since cigarette smoking creates many problems for the general public, it should be outlawed in all public places.

I. Harms health
    A. Lung disease
    B. Circulatory disease
II. Causes safety problems
    A. Destroys property
    B. Causes fires
III. Sanitation problems
    A. Soils the possessions
    B. Causes unpleasant odors
IV. Conclusion

Working Outline

A *working outline*, in contrast, is more fully fleshed out than a jotted outline. Expanded and divided into topics and subtopics, it helps you create a map as you draft your research paper. An effective working outline has the following parts:

- Introduction
- Thesis
- Major topics and subtopics
- Major transitions
- Conclusion

Usually, the entries are written as sentences.

Example of a Working Outline:
This outline was expanded from the previous jotted outline. Note that the entries are written as complete sentences.

Thesis: Since cigarette smoking creates many problems for the general public, it should be outlawed in all public places.

I. Cigarette smoke harms the health of the public.
    A. Cigarette smoke may lead to serious disease in nonsmokers.
        1. It leads to lung disease.
            a. It causes cancer.
            b. It causes emphysema.
        2. It leads to circulatory disease in nonsmokers.
            a. It causes strokes.
            b. It causes heart disease.

B. Cigarette smoke worsens other less serious health conditions.
  1. It aggravates allergies in nonsmokers.
  2. It causes pulmonary infections to become chronic.
  3. It can lead to chronic headache.
II. Cigarette smoking causes safety problems.
  A. Burning ash may destroy property.
  B. Burning cigarettes may cause serious fires.
III. Cigarette smoke leads to sanitation problems.
  A. Ash and tar soil the possessions of others.
  B. Ash and tar cause unpleasant odors and fog the air.
IV. Conclusions
  A. Cigarette smoking injures people's health and so should be banned in all public places.
  B. Cigarette smoking damages property and so should be banned in all public places.

Warning!

In general, a standard high school or college research paper should have no more than four or five main points. This means you shouldn't have more than four or five Roman numerals in your outline. If you have too many ideas, your paper is either too long or, more likely, vague and too general.

Now that you've whipped your material into shape, let's see about selecting the appropriate writing style to suit your audience, purpose, and topic. It's all covered in Chapter 13.

What Writing Style Do I Use?

*Wear your learning like your watch, in a private
pocket; do not merely pull it out and strike it;
merely to show you have one.*

LORD CHESTERFIELD

It's the moment of truth: time to start writing your first draft.
Even if you haven't finished all your research, once you complete most of your note cards and outline, it's time to start
writing. Drafting at this stage allows you to see what additional information you need so that you can fill it in. As you
begin to draft your paper, you must consider your writing
style.

Style

A writer's *style* is his or her distinctive way of writing. Style is
a series of choices—words, sentence length and structure, figures of speech, punctuation, and so on. The style you select for
your research paper depends on the following factors:

- Audience
- Purpose
- Tone

AUDIENCE

Knowing with *whom* you are communicating is fundamental to the success of any message. You need to tailor your writing style to suit the audience's needs, interests, and goals. The audience for your research paper is likely to be one of the following three people or groups:

- Your boss, supervisor, professor, teacher, instructor
- Your colleagues or classmates
- Any outside readers, such as clients

To tailor your research paper to your audience, do an audience analysis. Before you write, ask yourself these questions:

1. Who will be reading my research paper?
2. How much do my readers know about the topic at this point?
3. What is the basis of the information they have? (For example, reading, personal experience?)
4. How does my audience feel about this topic? Are they neutral, hostile, enthusiastic—or somewhere in between?
5. What style of writing does my audience anticipate and prefer?

PURPOSE

Writers have four main purposes:

- To explain (exposition)
- To convince (persuasion)
- To describe (description)
- To tell a story (narration)

In writing your research paper, your purpose is to *persuade*. As a result, select supporting material (such as details, examples, and quotations) that best accomplishes this purpose. As you write, look for the most convincing examples, the most powerful statistics, the most compelling quotations to suit your purpose.

TONE

The *tone* is the writer's attitude toward the subject matter.

Example:
The tone can be angry, bitter, neutral, or formal.

The tone depends on your audience and purpose. Since your research paper is being read by educated professionals and your purpose is to persuade, use a formal, unbiased tone. The writing should not condescend to the audience, insult them, or lecture them.

The language used in most academic and professional writing is called *Standard Written English,* the writing found in magazines such as *Newsweek, U.S. News & World Report,* and the *Atlantic.* Such language conforms to the widely established rules of grammar, sentence structure, usage, punctuation, and spelling. It has an objective, learned tone. It's the language to use in your research paper.

The Nitty-Gritty of Research Paper Style

WORDS

1. **Write simply and directly.** Perhaps you were told to use as many multisyllabic words as possible since "big" words dazzle people. Much of the time, however, big words just set up barriers between you and your audience. Instead of using words for the sake of impressing your readers, write simply and directly.

    Select your words carefully to convey your thoughts vividly and precisely.

    Example:
    "Blissful," "blithe," "cheerful," "contented," "gay," "joyful," and "gladdened" all mean "happy." Yet each one conveys a different shade of meaning.

2. **Use words that are accurate, suitable, and familiar.** *Familiar* words are easy to read and understand. *Accurate* words say what you mean. *Suitable* words convey your tone and fit with the other words in the document.

As you write your research paper, you want words that express the importance of the subject but aren't stuffy or overblown. Refer to yourself as *I* if you are involved with the subject, but always keep the focus on the subject rather than on yourself. Remember, this is academic writing, not memoir.

3. **Avoid slang, regional words, and nonstandard diction.** Here's a brief list of words that are never correct in academic writing:

Nonstandard Words and Expressions

Nonstandard	Standard
irregardless	regardless
being that	since
had ought	ought
could of	could have
this here	this
try and do	try to do
off of	off
that there	that

4. **Avoid redundant, wordy phrases.**

Examples:

Wordy	Concise
honest truth	truth
past history	history
fatally killed	killed
revert back	revert
true facts	facts
live and breathe	live
null and void	null (or void)
most unique	unique
cease and desist	cease (or desist)
proceed ahead	proceed

5. **Always use bias-free language.** Use words and phrases that don't discriminate on the basis of gender, physical condition, age, or race.

Example:

Avoid using "he" to refer to both men and women.

Never use language that denigrates people or excludes one gender.

Watch for phrases that suggest women and men behave in stereotypical ways, such as "talkative women."

In addition, always try to refer to a group by the term it prefers. Language changes, so stay on the cutting edge.

Example:

Today the term "Asian" is preferred to "Oriental."

SENTENCES

Effective writing uses sentences of different lengths and types to create variety and interest. Craft your sentences to express your ideas in the best possible way.

Guidelines:

1. Mix *simple, compound, complex,* and *compound-complex* sentences. When your topic is complicated or full of numbers, use simple sentences to aid understanding. Use longer, more complex sentences to show how ideas are linked and to avoid repetition. Check out the two sample papers at the end of this *Guide* for models.

2. Select the subject of each sentence based on what you want to emphasize.

3. Add adjectives and adverbs to a sentence (when suitable) for emphasis and variety.

4. Repeat key words or ideas for emphasis.

5. Use the active voice, not the passive voice.

6. Use transitions to link ideas.

PUNCTUATION

Similarly, successful research papers are free of technical errors.

Guidelines:

1. A period shows a full separation between ideas.

Example:

The car was in for repair Friday. I had no transportation to work.

2. A comma and a coordinating conjunction show the following relationships: addition, choice, consequence, contrast, or cause.

Example:
The car was in for repair Friday, but I still made it to work.

3. A semicolon shows that the second sentence completes the content of the first sentence. The semicolon suggests a link but leaves the connection to the reader.

Example:
The car was in for repair Friday; I didn't make work.

4. A semicolon and a conjunctive adverb (a word such as *nevertheless, however,* etc.) shows the relationship between ideas: addition, consequence, contrast, cause and effect, time, emphasis, or addition.

Example:
The car was in for repair Friday; however, I made it to work.

5. Using a period between sentences forces a pause and then stresses the conjunctive adverb.

Example:
The car was in for repair Friday. But I made it to work.

Warning!
Even if you run a grammar check in your word processor, check and double-check your punctuation and grammar as you draft your research paper.

Writing the Introduction

A research paper, like any good essay, starts off with an *introduction*. The introduction serves two purposes: It presents your thesis and gets the reader's attention. You can do this by means of:

- An anecdote (a brief story).
- A statement (usually the thesis).
- Statistics.
- A question.
- A quotation.

Select the method that suits your audience, purpose, and tone, as you have learned.

Example: Statement Used as an Introduction

Statement

To Edith Newbold Jones, *cross-currents with* English influences came early. Unlike other upper-middle-class New York ladies of the 1860s, young Edith grew deeply immersed in her father's impressive

Details

library on West 23rd Street. Her reading was mainly concentrated in English authors, for the only American literary works she perused were those of Prescott, Parkman, Longfellow, and Irving. As Louis Auchincloss maintains, culture and education, to

Source material

the Joneses, still meant Europe [Auchincloss 54].

Lead-in to second paragraph

Edith's education bears this out.

Here are other models for crafting the openings to your research papers. In each case, the specific technique is underlined.

Examples:

Anecdote

Anecdote ———

It was the game that could have ended a dynasty. There were only six seconds left on the clock. Seaford was up by one, but they were in trouble on their own 20-yard line without the ball against a powerful Bethpage. It was all up to the kicker to boot the ball through the uprights. The huddle broke and the whistle blew. The crowd jumped to their feet, hoping for a miracle. Thump! The ball flew high over the left upright. It didn't look good to the coaches, but the fans went wild. To the coaches' astonishment, the referee in the end zone signaled the kick was good. A look at the videotape told a different story, however. According to the camera, the ball wasn't clear.

Thesis statement ———

Instant replay could have changed the outcome of this crucial game—and many others like it on both local and national levels. That's why instant replay should be brought back to the NFL.

Statement

Statement —— Fifty years ago, two weeks after the blinding bang of a second atomic bomb burst and the riotous victory revelries, World War II formally passed into history on the deck of the battleship *Missouri.* Only a boatswain's piping punctuated the somber surrender ceremony. Once the last signature was completed, General Douglas MacArthur, the Allied commander, said, "These proceedings are closed." Succeeding generations of Japanese took that message to heart—particularly concerning their country's role as aggressor. But the passage of time has a way of prompting reflection.

Thesis statement —— Recently, Japan has undergone an astonishing aboutface.

Statistics

Statistic —— According to the National Highway Safety Administration, 1,136 lives have been saved by air bags between the years 1989 and 1995 [Reason 8]. Since 1991, an increasing number of auto manufacturers have equipped their cars with air bags. As the number of

Thesis statement —— cars equipped with air bags rises, so do the number of lives they save.

Question

An allegedly drunk driver runs down a person on a water scooter in the Great South Bay.
A Rocky Point teenager disappears in rough seas after going fishing in Lake Michigan in a Styrofoam boat lacking a sail, motor, or oars.
A speedboat with four people aboard strikes a rock and capsizes in high winds.

Questions —— Could these accidents have been avoided if the boat operator had acquired more boating skills? Would mandatory licensing for boat operators help prevent future tragedies? I believe that we must have both

Thesis statement —— mandatory safe boating education and licensing.

Quotation

Quotation ———— The ads trumpet, "You've come a long way, baby" but have we? Nothing could be further from the truth. Today, females have few positive role models, especially when it comes to the media. Television developers and

Thesis ———— producers have to take a long, hard look at the mes-
statement sages their programs send to the female population and rethink the format of current and future television shows.

In this chapter, you explored ways to suit your writing style to your audience, purpose, and tone. Now, find out how to use your source material to make your point.

Chapter 14

How Do I Use My Source Material?

*You could compile the worst book in the world
entirely out of selected passages from the
best writers in the world.*

G. K. CHESTERTON

Your purpose in any research paper is to use other people's words and ideas to support your thesis. Since you're not an authority on the subject you're writing about, you *must* rely on recognized experts to help you make your point. How can you smoothly blend source material with your own words? Follow the steps described in this chapter.

Use Cue Words and Phrases

How can you show that the material you are quoting, summarizing, and paraphrasing comes from outside sources and isn't something you made up? It's not enough just to plop the material into your paper, even if you surround exact quotes with quotation marks.

In addition to the awkwardness this creates, you're sacrificing most of the "punch" carried by expert opinions by not smoothly blending their words with yours. The reason for using outside sources is to buttress your claims, but if you're not going to give the experts clear credit in your research paper, you are in effect wasting their words.

Start by using *cue words* and phrases to set off outside material. As you blend the experts' words, be sure to include:

- The source of the material.
- The author's name.
- The author's identity, why this person is important. (This tells your readers why they should believe the person you cite.)
- The author's credentials, since they lend weight to the material.

Examples:

In *Shakespeare, the Comedies*, the noted literary critic Kenneth Muir claims that ...

In a March 15, 1999 front-page article in *The New York Times*, the well-known consumer activist Ralph Nader stated that ...

Testifying before Congress in 1985, prominent attorney F. Lee Bailey maintained that ...

Use the specific verb you need to indicate your exact shade of meaning. Here is a selection of verbs to choose from:

Verbs That Help You Integrate Quotations

adds	agrees	argues	concedes
acknowledges	admits	advises	confirms
asks	asserts	believes	concludes
claims	comments	compares	considers
contends	declares	defends	denies
disagrees	disputes	emphasizes	explain
endorses	grants	hints	hopes
finds	holds	illustrates	implies
insists	maintains	notes	observes
points out	rejects	relates	reports
responds	reveals	says	sees
speculates	shows	speculates	states
suggests	thinks	warns	writes

Document the Material

As you include the outside source, be sure to provide enough information for your readers to clearly understand where it comes from. In most cases, this is done through *parenthetical documentation, footnotes,* or *endnotes.* These are explained fully in Chapters 15 and 16.

Use the Material to Make Your Point

Never assume that your readers understand why you included information. You may appear to be simply padding your paper with lots of outside sources. To avoid this misunderstanding and to strengthen your point, clarify your message and focus on your argument. You can do this at the beginning or end of a passage.

Example:

Cue words	Feminist Gloria Steinem argues that "Employers adhere to a number of beliefs about women that serve to reinforce a pattern of non-employment and non-participation for female employees"
Parenthetical documentation	[Steinem 54]. Since many employers feel that women work for extra money, women's jobs are non-essential. This leads to the conclusion that men should
Your point	be hired or promoted rather than women.

Showing That Material Has Been Cut

What happens if a quotations contains material that's irrelevant to your point? You can use an *ellipsis* (three evenly spaced periods) to show that you have omitted part of a quotation.

You can use ellipses in the middle of a quotation or at the end. Do not use an ellipsis at the beginning of a sentence; just start with the material you wish to quote. If you omit more than one sentence, add a period before the ellipsis, to show that the omission occurred at the end of a sentence.

Example:
Readers of the *Atlantic Monthly* were astonished to find in the January 1875 issue the debut of one "Mark Twain." The originality of Twain's voice dazzled readers as the *Atlantic* showcased what was to become one of the great passages in American literature: "[Hannibal] the white town drowsing in the sunshine of a summer's morning" is shocked into life by the cry of "S-t-e-a-m-boat a-comin'!" As the Twain critic Justin Kaplan notes, "The gaudy packet ... was Mark Twain's reasserting his arrival and declaring once and for all that his surge of power and spectacle derived not from such streams as the meandering Charles or the sweet Thames but from 'the great Mississippi, the majestic, the magnificent Mississippi, rolling its mile-wide tide along, shining in the sun.'"

Warning!
Never omit material from a quotation to change its meaning deliberately. This is a sleazy way of slanting a quotation to make it say what you mean. In addition, always be sure that the quotation makes grammatical sense after you have cut it.

Who Gets Credit?

Sometimes you have an idea about your topic but find after researching that you weren't the first person to come up with this idea. To take credit for your original thinking but give credit to others who came up with the idea first, present both versions of the idea and give credit to the outside source. If necessary, explain how your idea is different from the reference you used.

Example:

Outside source | Since music fans have a great deal of difficulty obtaining tickets for certain concerts, any one customer should be prevented from buying more than four tickets at a time [Harvey 119]. However, this does not prevent scalpers from hiring "ringers" to

Author Page number

Your idea	stand in line and buy blocks of tickets. To overcome this problem, at least one-third of the tickets offered for sale should be set aside for bona fide students.

Setting Off Long Quotations

As mentioned earlier, try to avoid using long quotations in your research paper. But if you must quote more than four typed lines of text, follow these guidelines:

- Indent the quotation one inch from the left margin.
- Do not indent the right margin.
- Do not single-space the quotation; stay with double-spacing.
- Do not enclose the quotation in quotation marks; since it is offset, it is understood to be quoted.

As always, introduce the quotation with a sentence and cue words, usually followed by a colon (:).

Example:

In his book *Zen and the Art of Motorcycle Maintenance*, Robert Pirsig extends Twain's idea. As Pirsig explains:

◄—*1 inch*—►When analytic thought, the knife, is applied to experience, something is always killed in the process. Mark Twain's experience comes to mind, in which, after he had mastered the analytical knowledge needed to pilot the Mississippi River, he discovered the river had lost its beauty. Something is always killed. But what is less noticed in the arts—something is always created too. And instead of just dwelling on what is killed it's important also to see what's created and to see the process as a kind of death–birth continuity that is neither good nor bad, but just is [231-232].

Chapter 15

How Do I Cite My Sources?

Borrowed thoughts, like borrowed money, only show the poverty of the borrower.

MARGUERITE GARDINER

When you use someone else's words or ideas in your research paper, you *must* give credit. Otherwise, you're stealing their work. And whether the theft is intentional or accidental, the effect is the same: failure, humiliation, and perhaps even expulsion. Learn how to avoid literary theft by documenting your sources correctly.

What Is Plagiarism?

Plagiarism is the technical name for using someone else's words without giving adequate credit. Plagiarism is:

1. Using someone else's ideas without acknowledging the source.

2. Paraphrasing someone else's argument as your own.

3. Presenting someone else's line of thinking in the development of an idea as if it were your own.

4. Presenting an entire paper or a major part of it developed exactly as someone else's line of thinking.

5. Arranging your ideas exactly as someone else did—even though you acknowledge the source(s) in parentheses.

While plagiarism is a serious lapse in ethics as well as a cause for failure and even expulsion in some schools, documenting your sources correctly is easy. It also gives your research paper authority and credibility. Here's how to do it.

How Do I Avoid Plagiarism?

DOCUMENT QUOTATIONS

You must always set off direct quotes with quotation marks and give credit to your original source. It is considered plagiarism if you copy a part of the quotation without using quotation marks—even if you give credit.

Example:

Not Plagiarism

In a famous essay on the naturalists, Malcolm Cowley noted: "Naturalism has been defined in two words as *pessimistic determinism* and the definition is true as far as it goes. The naturalists were all determinists in that they believed in the omnipotence of abstract forces." [Becker 56]

Plagiarism

Malcolm Cowley defined Naturalism as "pessimistic determinism" and the definition is true as far as it goes. The naturalists were all determinists in that they believed in the omnipotence of abstract forces. [Becker 56]

DOCUMENT OPINIONS

You must also document the way an author constructs an argument or a line of thinking. In addition, it is considered plagiarism if you try to fob off someone else's opinions as your own.

Example:

Original Source

Probably the most influential novel of the era was *Uncle Tom's Cabin* (1852). More polemic than literature, *Uncle Tom's Cabin* nonetheless provided the North and South with the symbols and arguments they needed to get to war. [Levin 125]

Plagiarism

Uncle Tom's Cabin, published in 1852, was likely the most important novel of the pre-Civil War era. Even though the book was more a

116

debate than a novel, it nevertheless gave the Confederate and Union sides the push they needed to start the Civil War.

Not Plagiarism

As Harold Levin argues in his book *Roots of the Civil War, Uncle Tom's Cabin*, published in 1852, provided America with the impetus it need to plunge into the Civil War. Likely the most important novel of the era, *Uncle Tom's Cabin* cannot be regarded as "literature"—it is too strident for that. Nonetheless, its influence cannot be denied. [125]

DOCUMENT PARAPHRASES

The same holds true for paraphrases. It is not enough just to change a few words. Neither is it enough to rearrange a few sentences. Both practices can result in plagiarism.

Examples:

Original Source

William Dean Howells (1837-1920) was the most important literary figure in his time. In addition to championing many American writers such as Edith Wharton and Emily Dickinson, Howells promoted Ivan Turgenev, Leo Tolstoy, Henrik Ibsen, Emile Zola, George Eliot, and Thomas Hardy. [Goldsmith 98]

Plagiarism

William Dean Howells was the top literary person in his time. In addition to advancing the careers of American writers like Edith Wharton and Emily Dickinson, Howells championed the writing of non-Americans such as Ivan Turgenev, Leo Tolstoy, Henrik Ibsen, Emile Zola, George Eliot, and Thomas Hardy.

Not Plagiarism

William Dean Howells was the single most significant editor of his day. Howells helped the careers of Ivan Turgenev, Leo Tolstoy, Henrik Ibsen, Emile Zola, George Eliot, and Thomas Hardy as well as those of Edith Wharton and Emily Dickinson. [Goldsmith 98]

FACTS VS. COMMON KNOWLEDGE

By now you're probably thinking that you have to document every single word in your research paper—or pretty close! Not really. You have to document another person's words, ideas, or argument, and everything that is not common knowledge.

It's not difficult to document quotations, opinions, and paraphrases, but differentiating between facts and common knowledge can be tricky. *Common knowledge* is defined as the information an educated person is expected to know. People are expected to know general facts about many categories of common knowledge.

Examples:

Art	Geography	Mathematics
Computer science	History	Music
Cultural facts	Language	Science
Films	Literature	Social studies

How can you tell if something is common knowledge? If the fact is presented in several sources, odds are good that your readers are expected to know it. This means that you do not have to document it.

Examples of Common Knowledge

The Civil War started in 1861 and ended in 1865.

Abraham Lincoln was the president during that war.

He was assassinated by John Wilkes Booth.

Andrew Johnson became the new president.

In the following instance, however, the facts are *not* common knowledge and so have to be documented:

Example:

Original Source

By the time the last cannon thundered across the Shenandoah Valley at Antietam, the battlefield echoed with the screams of 20,000 Union and Confederate wounded. [Harris 415]

Plagiarism

When the last cannon roared at Antietam, 20,000 Union and Confederate wounded were left wounded across the Shenandoah Valley. They were yelling in excruciating pain.

Not Plagiarism

Antietam was one of the most devastating battles of the Civil War. By its conclusion, 20,000 Union and Confederate soldiers were wounded. [Harris 415]

MLA Documentation

There are several ways to document your sources. When you are writing in the humanities (English, history, social studies, etc.), you most often use the MLA style of *internal documentation*, a method created by the Modern Language Association. (In Chapter 16, you'll learn all about footnotes and endnotes.)

When you use internal documentation, you place as much of the citation as necessary within the text. The method makes it easy for your readers to track your sources as they read. Later, they can check your Works Cited page for a complete bibliographic entry. Internal documentation takes the place of traditional footnotes or endnotes.

What should you include in the body of the text? The first time you cite a work in your paper, include as much of the following information as necessary:

- The name of your source
- The writer's full name
- The writer's affiliation
- Page numbers

Example: Naming the Author
According to Van Wyck Brooks, Twain was a thwarted satirist whose bitterness toward the damned human race was the fruit of a lifelong prostitution of his talents. "The life of a Mississippi pilot had, in some special way, satisfied the instinct of the artist in him .... He felt that, in some way, he had been as a pilot on the right track; and he felt that he had lost this track" [252].

Example: Citing the Source
A recent *Time* magazine article, entitled "Video Madness," argues that small children become addicted to video games with devastating results [35].

Example: Omitting the Author or Author Unknown
The Long Island "greenbelt" is becoming seriously damaged by snowmobiles ("Destruction" 29).

Example: Citing an Indirect Source

Not everyone admired Twain's subjects or style. In a highly influential critical study, Van Wyck Brooks repeated Arnold Bennett's assessment of Twain as a "divine amateur" as well as Henry James' famous comment that Twain appeals to "rudimentary minds" [Brooks 21].

In the following chapter, you'll take this process one step further when you learn how to use footnotes and endnotes.

Chapter 16

How Do I Use Footnotes and Endnotes?

They lard their lean books with the fat of others' work.
ROBERT BURTON

Footnotes and endnotes are another form of documentation used in research papers. According to the *Chicago Manual of Style (CMS)*, *footnotes and endnotes* are often used in business, the fine arts, and the humanities to indicate the source of materials in a research paper.

In this chapter, you'll learn when and how to use footnotes and endnotes.

What Are Footnotes and Endnotes?

FOOTNOTES

A *footnote* is a bibliographic reference indicated by a number in the text. The complete citation is then placed at the bottom ("foot") of the same page.

Example:

Internal Documentation

Despite the increasing role of women in the workforce, most women remain in jobs traditionally defined as "women's work." Some employers see women as temporary fixtures in the labor force, predicting they will leave for reasons of marriage or child rearing. These employers tend to shuttle women into jobs where there is little or no room for advancement. [Thompson 65]

121

Footnote

Despite the increasing role of women in the workforce, most women remain in jobs traditionally defined as "women's work." Some employers see women as temporary fixtures in the labor force, predicting they will leave for reasons of marriage or child rearing. These employers tend to shuttle women into jobs where there is little or no room for advancement.[1]

[1]Roger Eggert, "Women's Economic Equality," *Time* 21 May 1995, 65.

ENDNOTES

An *endnote* is a bibliographic reference indicated by a number in the text. The complete citation is then placed at the end of the paper on a separate page labeled "Endnotes." An endnote is identical in form to a footnote, except that the full citation is placed at the end of the paper rather than at the bottom of the page.

Why Use Footnotes and Endnotes?

Use footnotes or endnotes in your research papers when you want to:

1. Document information without using internal documentation.
2. Add observations and comments that do not fit into your text.

As you learned in Chapters 14 and 15, most research papers in the humanities use internal documentation to give credit to sources. However, sometimes footnotes or endnotes are preferable to internal documentation. Use the method your audience or teacher prefers.

USING FOOTNOTES / ENDNOTES TO DOCUMENT SOURCES

Examples:

The dramatic increase in women's labor force participation has generated a great deal of public interest, resulting in both social and economic consequences.[1]

[1]Gregory Brown, *Women and Sex Roles: A Psychological Viewpoint* (New York: Dutton, 1997), 126.

As the women's movement gained momentum and two-income families became a necessity for attaining middle-class status, polls taken between 1972 and 1997 indicate that the approval of married women working outside the home has steadily increased.[2]

[2]Chris Siefert, "A Woman's Place is in the House—and Senate." *Ms.*, August 1997: 20.

USING FOOTNOTES / ENDNOTES TO ADD OBSERVATIONS AND COMMENTS

Whether you use internal documentation or footnotes/endnotes to give credit to outside sources, either type of note is useful for adding commentary, material that your reader will find useful but that doesn't directly pertain to your thesis. The footnote/endnote functions as a parenthetical comment, maintaining the flow of your paper.

Example:

Text of Paper

Carlos Baker's biography of *Ernest Hemingway: A Life Story* depicts his subject as a man of great complexity—volcanic, mercurial, frequently tortured.[18]

Footnote or Endnote

[18]The Woodrow Wilson Professor of Literature at Princeton University, Baker devoted seven years to the preparation of his acclaimed biography of Hemingway.

Guidelines for Using Footnotes/Endnotes

1. **Method.** Choose either endnotes or footnotes. Never use both in the same paper. In general, endnotes are easier to use than footnotes.

2. **Numbering.** Number footnotes or endnotes consecutively from the beginning to the end of your paper. *Do not* assign each source its own number or start with number 1 on each page. Use a new number for each citation even if several numbers refer to the same source.

3. **Placement in the text.** Place each citation number at the end of a direct or indirect quotation in the text.

Footnotes are placed on the bottom of the page on which they appear.

Endnotes are placed on a separate sheet of paper headed "Endnotes" or "Notes" at the end of your research paper.

4. **Format.** The numbers are superscript Arabic numerals (the numbers are raised a little above the words). Many computer programs set superscripts automatically. Single space each footnote, but double space between entries.

5. **Indenting.** Indent the first line of the footnote or endnote the same number of spaces as other paragraphs in your paper, usually five spaces. The second and all subsequent lines are placed "flush left" (to the left margin).

6. **Spacing.** Leave two spaces after the number at the end of a sentence. Don't leave any extra space before the number.

Footnote and Endnote Format

CITING BOOKS

The basic footnote/endnote citation for a book looks like this:

Footnote number. Author's First Name and Last Name, *Book Title* (Place of publication: Publisher, date of publication), page number.

Examples:
Book by One Author
[6]Phillip Roth, *Portnoy's Complaint* (New York: Random House, 1969), 231.

Part of a Book
[4]David Daiches, "Samuel Richardson," in *Twentieth Century Interpretations of Pamela,* ed. Rosemary Cowler (Englewood Cliffs, New Jersey: Prentice-Hall, 1969) 14.

Encyclopedia
[9]Funk and Wagnalls, 12th edition, "New Brunswick."

CITING PERIODICALS

The basic footnote/endnote citation for a magazine, newspaper, or journal looks like this:

Footnote number. Author's First Name and Last Name, "Article Title," *Periodical Title*, date, page number.

Examples:

Article in a Weekly or Monthly Magazine

[3]Trish Howard, "Babies Killing Babies," *Newsweek*, 16 July 1998, 23.

Review of a Book, Movie, or Play

[5]Nicole Padden, "Science Fiction or Science Fact?" Review of *Armageddon* (movie), *The Los Angeles Times*, 11 August 1998, 22A.

Signed Newspaper Article

To cite an unsigned newspaper title, begin with the title. Include all information that your reader might need to locate the source, such as the edition, section number or letter, and page number.

Example:

[22]Scott Sanders, "E-coli Poses Serious Threat to Travelers," *Washington Post*, 5 March 1998, Early City Edition, sec. 3, p. 6.

CITING ELECTRONIC SOURCES AND CD-ROMS

At the end of the entry, include the URL that you used to find the source as well as the name of the network.

Example:

[12]Macbeth. In *MIT Complete Works of Shakespeare*. Available from http://mitshakespeare.edu; INTERNET.

CITING GOVERNMENT DOCUMENTS

The basic footnote/endnote citation for a government document looks like this:

Footnote number. Government agency. Subsidiary agency. *Title of Document*. Individual Author, if included. (Publication information), page numbers.

Example:

[14]United States Congressional House Subcommittee on Health and Education, *Federal Policies Regarding Distribution of Aid to Dependent Children*. 97th Congress. (Washington, DC: GPO, 1995), 63.

CITING LECTURES OR SPEECHES

[13]Sharon Sorenson, "Addressing the Needs of the Learning-Disabled Middle-School Child" (Paper presented at the National Council of Teachers of English 1997 Annual Convention. Detroit, Michigan: 22 November, 1998).

CITING INTERVIEWS

[16]Meish Goldish, personal interview. 21 July 1998.

CITING TELEVISION OR RADIO SHOWS

[6]"AIDS Research," *20/20*. Narr. Barbara Walters, Prod. O. P. Malhotra, WABC, New York, 14 February 1997.

You now realize the importance of correctly documenting your sources, whether through internal documentation or footnotes/endnotes. The next chapter covers the next step in the process—creating a Works Cited page for the end of your research paper.

Chapter 17

How Do I Create a Works Cited Page?

A research paper is not a list of findings; it is the coherent communication of a meaningful pattern of information.

RICHARD COE

A *Works Cited* page list provides a complete citation for every work you *cited* in your research paper. A *Bibliography* (or *Works Consulted* list), in contrast, provides a full citation for every work you *consulted* as you wrote your paper.

In most scholastic research papers, instructors require a Works Cited page. However, in business or another environment you may be asked to prepare a Bibliography/Works Consulted list as well. Be sure you know what you're required to submit with your research paper.

MLA Citation Format

The standard MLA citation formats follow. Remember to use MLA-style formatting for papers in the humanities.

CITING BOOKS

The basic citation for a book looks like this:

Author's Last Name, First Name. *Book Title.* Place of publication: Publisher, date of publication.

Book with One Author

Example:

Hartz, Paula. *Abortion: A Doctor's Perspective, a Woman's Dilemma.* New York: Donald I. Fine, Inc., 1992.

Book with Two or More Authors

Notice that the first author's name is inverted for alphabetical order.

Example:

Landis, Jean M. and Rita J. Simon. *Intelligence: Nature or Nurture?* New York: HarperCollins, 1998.

Book with Four or More Authors

You can cite all the authors listed or only the first one and then write *et al.* ("and others") for the rest of the authors.

Example:

Frieze, Irene H., et. al. *Women and Sex Roles: A Psychological Perspective.* New York: W.W. Norton & Company, Inc., 1978.

Corporation

Give the name of the corporation as the author, even if it is the publisher as well.

Example:

People for the Ethical Treatment of Animals. *Animal Rights.* New York: PETA, 1995.

Author and an Editor

Include the author's name, the title of the book, and then the editor. Use the abbreviation *Ed.* whether there is one editor or many.

Example:

Nathaniel Hawthorne. *Nathaniel Hawthorne's Tales.* Ed. James Macintosh. New York: W.W. Norton & Company, Inc., 1987.

Editor

Give the name of the editor or editors, followed by *ed.* (if one editor) or *eds.* (if more than one editor).

Example:

Ellmann, Richard and Robert O'Clair, eds. *The Norton Anthology of Modern Poetry.* New York: W.W. Norton & Company, Inc., 1988.

Book in a Series

After the title, include the name of the series and series number.

Example:

Spencer, Charles. *Ernest Hemingway.* Twayne's United States Authors Series 54. Boston: Twayne, 1990.

Translation

After the title, write *Trans.* ("translated by") and the name of the translator.

Example:

Voltaire. *Candide or l'optimisme.* Trans. George R. Havens. New York: Holt, Rinehart and Winston, 1969.

Selection Reprinted in Anthology

First give the name of the author and the title of selection, then the title of the book, the editor, the edition, and the publication information.

Example:

Mailer, Norman. "Censorship and Literary Cowardice." *Lend Me Your Ears: Great Speeches in History.* Ed. William Safire. New York: W.W. Norton & Company, Inc., 1992.

CITING PERIODICALS

The basic citation for an article looks like this:

Author's Last Name, First Name. "Title of the Article." *Magazine.* Month and year of publication: page numbers.

Note on Numbers:

- If the page numbers in an article are not consecutive, cite the first page number followed by a plus sign (+).

- The date in a bibliographic citation is written in European style, with the date *before* the month, rather than *after.*

Example:

12 September 1989

Here are some models to show you the variations on periodical citations.

Article in Monthly Magazine

Example:

Crowley. J. E., T. E. Levitan and R. P. Quinn. "Seven Deadly Half-Truths about Women." *Psychology Today*, March 1978: 94-106.

Article in Weekly Magazine

Example:

Schwartz, Felice N. "Management, Women, and the New Facts of Life." *Newsweek*, 20 July 1998: 21-22.

Signed Newspaper Article

Example:

Ferraro, Susan. "In-law and Order: Finding Relative Calm." *The Daily News*, 30 June 1998: 73.

Unsigned Newspaper Article

Example:

"Beanie Babies May Be a Rotten Nest Egg." *Chicago Tribune*, 21 June 1989: 12.

Editorial

Show that the article is an editorial by writing *Editorial* after the title.

Example:

"Dealing with the National Debt." Editorial. *Newsday*, 12 October 1998, sec. 2:4.

Review

To indicate that an article is a book, movie, or play review, write *Rev. of* before the work being reviewed. Use the abbreviation *dir.* for the director.

Example:

Barnes, Clive. "The Story of a Life." Rev. of *Collected Stories*, dir. Liz Uslan. *The New York Times*, 1 August 1998: 34-35.

CITING ELECTRONIC SOURCES AND CD-ROMS

Electronic sources are often missing key information such as the author and date. Use whatever information you can find.

Since electronic sources are updated often, the citations can change without notice—even from the time you use them to the time you create your Works Cited page! Again, try to get the most up-to-date information but recognize that this may not always be possible.

That said, here are some models.

Periodicals Available on Both CD-ROM and in Print

Include in your citation all the information you would for a print magazine, as well as:

- The publication medium (CD-ROM).
- The name of the distributor or vendor.
- The electronic publication date.

Example:
Moon, William Least Heat. "Blue Highways." *U.S. News & World Report,* 17 January 1993: 12+. Native American Voices. CD-ROM. InfoTrak. March 1998.

Periodicals Available Only on CD-ROM
Include:

- Author.
- Title.
- Edition.
- Publication medium (CD-ROM).
- Distributor or vendor.
- City of publication.
- Publisher.
- Date of publication.

Example:
"Dinosaurs." *Compton's Interactive Encyclopedia.* 1995 ed. CD-ROM. Cambridge, Massachusetts, 1997.

On-Line Sources
These include materials available through America On-line, CompuServe, Prodigy, Dialog, Nexis, and other services. For these sources, give:

- Author's name (if available).
- Title of the source.

- Publication date.
- Database.
- Publication medium (on-line).
- Name of the computer service.
- Date of access.

Example:
Henry, Veronica. "Snorkeling in the Great Barrier Reef." *New York Times*: A6. 1 February 1995. *New York Times Online*. On-line. Prodigy 12 April 1998.

Electronic News Groups and Bulletin Boards
Include:

- Author's name.
- Title of the document.
- Date the source was posted.
- Medium (on-line posting).
- Location online.
- Name of the network.
- Date of access.

Example:
Brown, Margery. "Inclusion of Handicapped Children." 20 March 1997. On-line posting. ivillage, Children with Special Needs. America Online 25 March 1997.

E-mail
Give:

- Sender's name.
- Description of the document.
- Date of the document.

Example:
Lawrence, Charles. "Fair Division." E-mail to Jill Fitzpatrick. 26 May 1996.

CITING PAMPHLETS

Cite a pamphlet the same way you would a book, but the pamphlet title is enclosed in quotes, not italicized.

Jaffe, Natalie. "Men's Jobs for Women: Toward Occupational Equality." *Public Affairs Pamphlet* 606 (August 1968): 10-17.

CITING GOVERNMENT DOCUMENTS

The format varies with the information available. The basic citation for a government document looks like this:

Government agency. Subsidiary agency. *Title of Document.* Publication information.

Examples:

U.S. Department of Labor Statistics, 1997.

United States Congressional House Subcommittee on Health and Education. *Federal Policies Regarding Distribution of Aid to Dependent Children.* 97th Congress. Washington, DC: GPO, 1995.

CITING LECTURES OR SPEECHES

Include:

- Speaker.
- Title of the speech.
- Name of the occasion or sponsoring organization.
- Location.
- Date.

If you can't get all this information, provide as much as possible.

Example:

Sorenson, Sharon. "Addressing the Needs of the Learning-Disabled Middle-School Child." National Council of Teachers of English Annual Convention. Detroit, Michigan: 22 November, 1998.

CITING INTERVIEWS

Name the subject of the interview, followed by *Personal interview* or *Telephone interview*. Then comes the date.

Example:

Goldish, Meish. Personal interview. 21 July 1998.

Identify significant people involved with the production, followed by their role:

- *Writ.* (writer)
- *Dir.* (director)
- *Perf.* (performer)
- *Narr.* (narrator)
- *Prod.* (producer)

Example:
"AIDS Research." *20/20.* Narr. Barbara Walters. Prod. O.P. Malhotra. WABC, New York, 14 February 1997.

Page Format

The Works Cited page (or the Bibliography) is the last page of your paper. Here are some additional guidelines to follow as you prepare this page:

1. **Title.** Center the title "Works Cited" at the top of the page, about one inch from the top. Do not underline it, boldface it, or place it in italics.
2. **Alphabetical order.** Entries are arranged in alphabetical order according to the first author's last name. If the entry does not have an author (such as an encyclopedia entry or an editorial), alphabetize it according to the first word of the title. Ignore the prepositions "A," "An," and "The."
3. **Numbering.** Do not number the entries.
4. **Indentation.** Start each entry flush left. Don't indent it, but do indent the second and all subsequent lines of an entry. Use the standard indent of five spaces.
5. **Spacing.** As in the rest of your paper, double space each entry on your Works Cited page.

So you've learned how to construct a Works Cited page. That means it's show time! In the next chapter, you'll learn how to present your research paper.

Chapter 18

How Do I Present My Research Paper?

*The ink of the scholar is more sacred than the
blood of the martyr.*

MUHAMMAD

If you've gotten this far, you're in the home stretch! Just a
few more matters to attend to and you'll be ready to hand in
your research paper. Now it's time to consider the material
that comes before the body of your paper (the *frontmatter*)
and the material that comes after (the *endmatter*). It's also
time to learn how to present your paper, including typing
and binding.

Frontmatter

Depending on the subject of your research paper and the
course requirements, you may need to include specific materials before the body of your paper, such as:

- Title page
- Table of contents
- Foreword
- Preface
- Abstract

Always check with whoever requested the paper (instructor, supervisor, etc.) to see if you are required to include frontmatter and, if so, which elements. Requirements vary, even from assignment to assignment.

TITLE PAGE

Most high school and college research papers require a title page. Your title page should contain:

- The title.
- Your name.
- The name of the course.
- Your instructor's name.
- The date.

Here's how to arrange the information:

- **Title.** Center the title one-third down the page. Repeat the title on the first page, centered on the first line. Doublespace between the title and the first line of the text.
- **Your name.** Place your name half-way down the page, prefaced by the word "by."
- **Course name, instructor's name, date.** These go directly under your name. Double space between lines.

If a title page is not required, your first page functions as a title page.

TABLE OF CONTENTS

The *table of contents* lists the main divisions of your paper. If you include a table of contents, label each section of the paper to match the headings on your table of contents. The table of contents appears directly after the title page. Type it last so that you can enter the page numbers.

FOREWORD AND PREFACE

Including a foreword or preface in a high school or college research paper is unusual. In business or other environments, a short foreword or preface might be appropriate. In most cases:

- The *foreword* is written by an expert in the field and serves as an endorsement of the contents.
- The *preface,* written by the author of the paper, explains how the paper came to be written and gives thanks to people who helped with research and other related matters.

ABSTRACT

An *abstract* is a brief summary of the paper's contents. Objective in tone, abstracts are often included in technical or scholarly papers. An abstract usually runs 100 to 125 words. It is presented on a separate page in one to two paragraphs. Do not indent the first line. The title is provided to make it easier for you to understand the topic.

Example of Abstract

How the Division within the Liberal Community was Reflected in the Nation, 1930–1950

Granville Hicks charged in the New Masses in 1937 that the Nation had abandoned its long-held position as unofficial organ of the Liberal Left when it deliberately selected anti-Stalinist reviewers for books dealing with Soviet Russia. The Nation called the charges unjustified. Fourteen years later, Hicks once again attacked the Nation, this time charging that the editorial section gave the Russians the benefit of every doubt.

Hicks was correct in his charges and in this see-saw of beliefs and allegiances lies the main story of our time. The initial pull of Communism, drawing away, and resulting breakup of the Left determined the literary course of American radicalism.

Endmatter

VISUALS

Visuals include graphs, charts, maps, graphs, figures, and photographs. You can draw them by hand or prepare them on a computer. Place each graphic at the appropriate place in the text or group them at the end.

Visuals that you did not create yourself must be credited the same way you would credit any outside source.

GLOSSARY

A *glossary* lists and defines technical terms or presents additional information on the subject.

Example:
If you are writing a research paper on Shakespeare, you might include a brief glossary of Shakespearean English, a glossary of films that tie in with the topic, or a glossary of notable Shakespearean actors or performances.

Presentation Format

Research papers follow a standard presentation format. They are *never* submitted in handwritten form. In an academic environment, if you cannot keyboard your paper, speak to your instructor well in advance of the paper's due date.

Follow these format guidelines:

1. **Paper stock.** Use white paper, standard $8^{1}/_{2} \times 11$-inch size. If you use continuous-form paper, be sure to remove the perforated edges, separate the pages, and place them in the correct order.

2. **Fonts.** Use standard 10- or 12-point fonts in Times Roman, Courier, or Helvetica. Avoid fancy, elaborate fonts, since they are difficult to read.

3. **Formatting.** Avoid stylistic elements that might distract readers, such as excessive highlighting, boldfacing, or boxes.

4. **Spacing.** Double space the text. Leave a $1^{1}/_{2}$-inch margin on the left side and 1 inch on the other sides.

5. **Justification.** Do not justify (right-align) your paper. The right margins should be ragged. Your word processor automatically justifies your left margin.

6. **Pagination.** Number each page and write your name in the upper right-hand corner. Do not place a number on

the title page, but count it in the final number of pages you submit. Most computer software programs can create an automatic page header. This inserts your name and the page number automatically on each page.

7. **Indenting.** Indent five spaces at the beginning of each paragraph.

8. **Punctuation and word breaks.** Never begin a line with a comma, colon, semicolon, dash, or any type of end punctuation. Break words at syllables; do not divide words of five letters or fewer.

9. **Order of pages.** Arrange your pages in this order:

    Title page (if required)

    Outline (if required)

    The body of the paper

    Any relevant backmatter

    Works Cited

10. **Binding.** Check with your instructor or supervisor for specific guidelines.

    Examples:
    In a folder
    Stapled
    Paperclipped

Additional Guidelines

Every scholarly field has a preferred style of presentation. Here are some of the standard style manuals for different fields.

- **Biology.** Council of Biology Editors. *Scientific Style and Format: The CBE Manual for Authors, Editors, and Publishers,* 6th edition. New York: Cambridge University Press, 1994.

- **Chemistry.** American Chemical Society. *The SCS Style Guide: A Manual for Authors and Editors.* Washington, DC: ACS, 1985.

- **English and the humanities:** Gibaldi, Joseph. *MLA Handbook for Writers of Research Papers,* 4th edition. New York: Modern Language Association, 1995.

- **Engineering:** Michaelson, Herbert B. *How to Write and Publish Engineering Papers and Reports,* 3rd edition. Phoenix, Arizona: Oryx, 1990.

- **Geology:** United States Geological Survey. *Suggestions to Authors of the Reports of the United States Geological Survey,* 7th edition. Washington, DC: GPO, 1991.

- **Law.** *The Bluebook: A Uniform System of Citation.* Comp. Editors of Columbia Law Review et al. 15th edition. Cambridge: Harvard Law Review, 1991.

- **Linguistics.** Linguistic Society of America. *LSA Bulletin,* December issue, annually.

- **Mathematics.** American Mathematical Society. *A Manual for Authors of Mathematical Papers,* 8th rev. edition. Providence: AMS, 1990.

- **Medicine.** Iverson, Cheryl, et al. *American Medical Association Manual of Style.* 8th edition. Baltimore: Williams, 1989.

- **Music.** Holoman, D. Kern, ed. *Writing about Music: A Style Sheet from the Editors of 19th-Century Music.* Berkeley: University of California Press, 1988.

- **Physics.** American Institute of Physics. *AIP Style Manual,* 4th edition. New York: AIP, 1990.

- **Psychology.** American Psychological Association. *Publication Manual of the American Psychological Association,* 4th edition. Washington: APA, 1994.

Presentation *does* matter! That's why you'll next learn about revising, editing, and proofreading your research paper.

Part IV

Writing the Final Copy

Chapter 19

How Do I Revise, Edit, and Proofread?

The difference between the right word and the nearly right word is the same as that between ightning and the lightning bug.

MARK TWAIN

Revising

When you think "revising," think "rewriting." Your first draft rarely says all you want to say, in the best possible way. Experienced writers know that it takes several drafts to convey your meaning clearly. This is especially true when you're writing a research paper, where outside material is used to support your thesis.

Here are some guidelines to follow as you revise:

- Give your writing time to sit and "cool off" between drafts. Problems often become much clearer if you let some time elapse between writing and revision.

- Allow sufficient time for revision. It's not unusual to spend as much time revising as writing—if not more!

- Don't be afraid to make significant changes as you revise. You will likely change the order of paragraphs, delete sections, and add new passages.

- Save successive drafts of your documents in different computer files, such as paper1.doc, paper2.doc, paper3.doc, and so on. You might find a use for deleted material later.
- Share your writing with others. Peer reviewers can often help you spot areas that need revision. Consider their comments carefully.
- If your school or university has a Writing Center, have them help revise your paper, too.

Editing

Use the following checklist as you edit your paper:

_____ Is my writing *accurate*?

_____ Are my sentences *concise* and to the point?

_____ Have I included sufficient *detail*? Does my paper have all the information and explanation I need to support the thesis?

_____ Do I *prove my thesis*?

_____ Do I use the level of *diction* appropriate for my audience?

_____ Is my writing *coherent*? Do I link related ideas with transitions?

_____ Does my writing have a clear *voice*? Is the voice appropriate to the subject and audience?

_____ Have I *given credit* to each source? Have I avoided plagiarism?

_____ Is my paper in the correct *form*, including a title page, outline, Works Cited page, or anything else required by the assignment?

_____ Is my writing *correct*? Have I used the correct grammar, spelling, and punctuation?

Proofreading

As you prepare your final draft, proofread it carefully to catch any typos or other errors. Read your draft aloud, very slowly, saying each word. Use a ruler or piece of paper to guide your eyes to make sure you don't skip any words. Try reading your paper *backwards* to help you focus on each word. It's also helpful to ask one or more people to proofread your paper as well.

Correcting Misused Words

Too many errors in spelling, punctuation, and grammar can harm an otherwise competent research paper and seriously affect your grade.

Spell checkers are very useful inventions, but they have several shortcomings. They're useless when it comes to homonyms and homophones.

- *Homonyms* are words with the same spelling and pronunciations but different meanings.

  Example:
  Beam and beam

- *Homophones* are words with the same pronunciation but different spellings and meanings.

  Example:
  Coarse and course

As a result, you must proofread your paper carefully to catch misused words. This is crucial because it helps you write exactly what you mean. English has a lot (not allot) of these confusing words. Use the following list as a guide as you edit and revise your research paper.

THE 60 MOST OFTEN CONFUSED WORDS

1. *accept*: to take
   except: to leave out, to exclude

2. *advise*: to give counsel
   advice: counsel
3. *air*: atmosphere
   err: to make a mistake
4. *affect*: to influence (verb)
   affect: a psychological state (noun)
   effect: impact and purpose (noun)
   effect: to bring about (verb)
5. *a lot*: many
   allot: to divide
6. *altar*: a platform on which religious rites are performed
   alter: to change
7. *allowed*: permitted
   aloud: out loud, verbally
8. *all together*: all at one time
   altogether: completely
9. *allude*: to refer to
   elude: to escape
10. *already*: previously
    all ready: completely prepared
11. *allusion*: a reference to a place, event, person, work of art, or other work of literature
    illusion: a misleading appearance or a deception
12. *among*: three or more people, places, or things
    between: two people, places, or things
13. *amount*: things that <u>can't</u> be counted
    number: things that <u>can</u> be counted
14. *arc*: part of the circumference of a circle; curved line
    ark: boat
15. *are*: plural verb
    our: belonging to us

16. *ascent*: a move up
    assent: to agree
17. *bare*: undressed, uncovered
    bare: unadorned, plain
    bear: fuzzy-wuzzy animal
    bear: to carry, to hold
18. *base*: the bottom part of an object; first, second, or third in baseball; morally low
    bass: the lowest male voice; a type of fish; a musical instrument
19. *beau*: sweetheart
    bow: to bend from the waist (verb)
    bow: a device used to propel arrows (noun); loop of ribbon (noun); the forward end of a ship (noun)
20. *berth*: a sleeping area in a ship
    birth: being born
21. *board*: a thin piece of wood; a group of directors
    bored: not interested
22. *born*: native, brought forth by birth
    borne: endured (past participle of "to bear")
23. *bore*: tiresome person
    boar: male pig
24. *brake*: a device for slowing a vehicle
    break: to crack or destroy
25. *bread*: baked goods
    bred: to cause to be born
26. *breadth*: the side-to-side dimension
    breath: inhalation and exhalation
27. *bridal*: pertaining to the bride or a wedding
    bridle: part of a horse's harness
28. *buy*: to purchase
    by: near or next to

29. *capital*: the city or town that is the official seat of government; highly important; net worth of a business

capitol: the building housing the seat of government

30. *conscience*: moral sense

conscious: awake

31. *cell*: a small room, as in a convent or prison

sell: to trade

32. *cent*: a penny

scent: aroma

33. *cheep*: what a bird says

cheap: not expensive

34. *deer*: animal

dear: beloved

35. *do*: to act or make (verb)

due: caused by (adjective)

36. *draft*: breeze; a stage of preparation of written work

draft: to sketch or prepare

37. *dye*: change color

die: to cease living

38. *emigrate*: to move away from one's country

immigrate: to move to another country

39. *eminent*: distinguished

imminent: expected momentarily

immanent: inborn, inherent

40. *fare*: price charged for transporting a passenger

fair: not biased; moderately large; moderately good

41. *faze*: to stun

phase: a stage

42. *for*: because

four: the number 4

43. *gorilla*: ape

guerrilla: soldier

44. *grate*: to irritate, reduce to small pieces (verb)
    grate: metal lattice (noun)
    great: big, wonderful
45. *hair*: the stuff on your head
    heir: beneficiary
46. *here*: in this place
    hear: to listen
47. *hours*: 60-minute period
    ours: belonging to us
48. *it's*: contraction for "it is"
    its: possessive pronoun
49. *lay*: to put down
    lie: to be flat
50. *lead*: to conduct
    lead: bluish-gray metal
    led: past tense of "to lead"
51. *loose*: not tight, not fastened (noun)
    loose: to untighten, to let go (verb)
    lose: to misplace (verb)
52. *meat*: animal flesh
    meet: encounter; proper
53. *peace*: calm
    piece: part
54. *plain*: not beautiful; obvious
    plane: airplane
55. *presence*: company, closeness
    presents: gifts
56. *principal*: main; head of a school
    principle: rule
57. *reed*: plants
    read: to interpret the written word

58. *right*: correct
   write: to form letters
59. *than*: comparison
   then: at that time
60. *their*: belonging to them
   they're: contraction for "they are"
   there: place

SPELL IT ~~RITE~~ ~~WRIGHT~~ RIGHT

Learning standard spelling rules can serve you well as you proofread your research papers. Here are the basics:

i before e except after c, or as sounded as a as in neighbor and weigh

Examples: Words That Fit the Rule

i before e	except after *c*	sounded as *a*
achieve	conceit	neighbor
believe	ceiling	weigh
siege	receive	freight
relief	conceive	reign
grief	deceit	sleigh
chief	deceive	vein
fierce	perceive	weight
fiend	receipt	beige
piece	receive	eight
shriek		feint
bier		heir
yield		surveillance
relieve		veil
piece		

Examples: Words That Don't Fit the Rule

either	neither	foreign	height
leisure	seize	weird	protein
codeine	financier	glacier	counterfeit
	Fahrenheit	fiery	

e, i, e, i (no o)

Words with *i* and *e* pronounced with a long *a* sound are always spelled *-ei*, never *-ie*.

Examples:

eight	feign	sleigh
vein	neigh	peignoir

If the sound is a long *i*, the word is usually spelled with the *-ei* combo, not *-ie*.

Examples:

feisty
stein
seismic
height
leitmotif

Common Exceptions:

hierarchy
fiery
hieroglyphic

Notice that in each case, the *-ie* combination is followed by an *r*.

Last, *ie* words with a short vowel sound usually spell it *-ie* rather than *-ei*.

Examples:

patient
friend
transient
sieve
mischief
handkerchief

Exceptions:

heifer
nonpareil
sovereign
counterfeit
surfeit

The -ceed/-cede Rule

Only three verbs in English end in *-ceed*:

succeed

proceed

exceed

All the other verbs with that sound end in *-cede*.

Example
secede
recede
intercede
concede
accede
cede
precede

The -ful Rule

Remember that the sound *full* at the end of a word is spelled with only one *l*.

Examples:

Root Word	+	Suffix	=	New Word
care	+	ful	=	careful
grace	+	ful	=	graceful
hope	+	ful	=	hopeful

When the suffix is *-ful* plus *-ly*, there are two *l*s.

Examples:

Root Word	+	Suffix	=	New Word
restful	+	ly	=	restfully
thankful	+	ly	=	thankfully
zestful	+	ly	=	zestfully

-ery or -ary?

Only six commonplace words end with *-ery* as opposed to *-ary*:

cemetery

confectionery

millinery

monastery

distillery

stationery (writing paper)

Q Followed by u

This is a nice rule, because it has only one English exception, the lightweight nylon fabric called *Qiana*. The rule doesn't fit with abbreviations or foreign words, however.

Example:

The abbreviation for *quart* is *qt.* (not *qut.*)
The east Arabia peninsula on the Persian Gulf is *Qatar*, not *Quatar*, but that's OK, because the word can also be spelled *Katar*.

ks and cs

Some words that end in c have a hard *k* sound. Adding *y, i,* or *e* after the final *c* changes the hard sound to a soft one, creating spelling dilemmas. As a general rule, add a *k* after the final *c* when the hard sound becomes soft.

Examples:

Word Ending in C	Adding the K
mimic	mimicked, mimicking, mimicker
traffic	trafficked, trafficking, trafficker
panic	panicked, panicking, panicky

Compound Words

Compound words fall into three categories: open compounds, closed compounds, hyphenated compounds.

Open compounds are written as two words:

Examples:

cedar shingles   night shift   executive secretary

Closed compounds are written as one word:

Examples:

handbook   northeast   homemaker

Hyphenated compounds have a hyphen:

Examples:

comparison-contrast   nurse-practitioner

Warning!

A *hyphen* is one click of the button (-); a dash is two (--). A hyphen is used *within* words; a dash is used *between* words.

PROOFREADING SYMBOLS

What happens if you have completely finished proofreading your paper, you print it out, and while you're waiting to hand it in, you suddenly spot a few more errors? Don't panic! If there are only a few errors, mark them with the following proofreading symbols rather than retyping an entire page, or racing back to the computer, or interrupting the clerical assistant *again*.

Proofreading Marks

Lowercase	*lc*	Period	⊙
Capital letter	*cap or*	Comma	∧
Close up space	*#, or* ⌒	Colon	⊙⋀
Insert space	∧#	Semicolon	∧;
Paragraph	ℙ	Question mark	**?**
No paragraph	*no* ℙ	Apostrophe	∨
Delete	↗	Open quotes	ⱽⱽ
Delete and leave one space	↗ *or* #↗	Close quotes	ⱽⱽ
Delete and close up	⌒	Hyphen	|=|
Let it stand	(*stet*)	Dash	$\frac{1}{N}$, $\frac{1}{M}$, $\frac{2}{M}$, $\frac{3}{M}$
Flush left, right	[ ]	Parentheses	ɟ ɟ
Brackets	ɟ ɟ	Move right or left	← →
Center	] [	Transpose	⌣⌢
Align horizontally	⥾	Insert letter	∧
Align vertically	≋	Underscore	*u.s.*
Boldface	∿∿∿	Italic	_____

The final chapter contains two model papers. Study them for form, especially how the writers introduce the thesis statement, lay out the points to be covered, move smoothly from point to point, and handle citations.

Chapter 20

Model Papers

Use the following research papers as guidelines as you prepare your own.

Model #1: Comics and History

Outline

Thesis: The development of comic books reflected the social situations of the 20th century.

I. 1930s: Comics offer escapism from the Depression.
   A. Escapist fantasies fuel comic strips.
   B. Comic strips compiled into books.
   C. Golden Age of Comics began.
II. 1940–1945: Comics serve as American propaganda in World War II.
   A. WW II brings escapism, reflected in comics.
   B. Comics feature patriotic heroes fighting for American values.
III. 1946–1950: Comics languished.
   A. The atomic bomb eclipsed superheroes' impact.
   B. "Archie" comics become popular with America's teenagers.
   C. Horror comics appear; become increasingly gory.
IV. 1950–1955: Comics fall prey to Congressional attack.
   A. Congress meets to determine if juvenile delinquency caused by comics.
   B. Comics Code Authority formed to censor objectionable material in comics.
V. 1956–1960s: Superheroes return to comics.
   A. New superheroes mirror American quest for heroes.

B. War comics show civilian side of conflict, reflecting America's conflicting feelings about the Vietnam War.
VI. 1970s: Comics again became relevant.
  A. Comics focus on important issues in the 1970s.
  B. Comics become more gritty and realistic.
VII. 1990s: Comics reflect modern concerns.
  A. Comics keyed to pressing social issues.
  B. Comics similar to TV and movies in themes and topics.

Comics and History

During the 1930s, purveyors of popular culture offered escape to the American people. Their efforts served in part to ease people through the economic calamity of the Depression. Comic strips such as "Tarzan," "Buck Rogers," and "Prince Valiant" served to transport the reader elsewhere—a jungle, a desert, a distant planet, the past or the future—where the action had no bearing on the grueling reality of the day. As the decade progressed, adventure strips grew in popularity, fueling escapist fantasies for the economically distressed [Savage 3].

The comic book industry began in the mid-1930s. Publisher M. C. "Max" Gaines thought that compiling a collection of newspaper comic strips in a magazine form would work well as a premium giveaway [Thompson 23]. So the first comic book was just that, reprints, given away with products ranging from soap to breakfast cereal to children's shoes. Other companies quickly saw the popularity of such magazines and very soon, all the usable strips were being reprinted and sold as books [Savage 4].

In 1934, Major Malcolm Wheeler-Nicholson started his company by printing *New Comics* and *New Fun Comics*, using all new material. He hired Max Gaines to be in charge. In 1936, they started another new title, *Detective Comics*, the first comic book devoted to a single theme. These were precursors to the vaunted "golden age" of comic books.

The so-called "Golden Age" of comics officially began in 1938. While looking for a lead feature to launch another new title, Gaines and his editors settled on a strip that had been created five years earlier and unsuccessfully offered as a newspaper strip by two teenagers from Cleveland, Jerry Seigel and Joe Shuster. The character could lift cars, leap over buildings, and bounce bullets off his chest. The new magazine was named *Action Comics*. The character was called Superman [Daniels 32].

Superman proved to be an overnight success. As quickly as they could, other publishers--and DC itself, as Gaines' company had come to be called--sought to make economic lightning strike again and again. Costumed heroes arrived by the busload, feeding the escapist public with fantastic adventures [Savage 17].

Not long before the second World War, impelled by world affairs and the public mood, the comic book industry created a number of "patriotic" heroes: Captain America, Fighting Yank, The Americommando, and even Uncle Sam, who began appearing in *National Comics* in July of 1940. This signaled the end of comic book escapism. As war became part of everyday life, comics became a vehicle for propaganda.

Military Comics was launched several months before the United States entered World War II, advertising "Stories of the Army and Navy." The leading hero was Blackhawk who, we learned in the first issue, was a Polish aviator whose family had been killed by Nazis. He waged aerial guerrilla warfare against Nazi Germany in his distinctive

4

Blackhawk plane--which had a striking resemblance to a Grumman skyrocket [Goulart 181].

Comic books became a part of the Allied propaganda machine, emphasizing the need for a maximum war effort by portraying the enemy as a vast, inhuman evil. All variety of heroes, including Superman and Batman, were portrayed on covers promoting war bonds and punching out the "JapaNazis." Additionally, hundreds of thousands of comics were shipped to Allied troops around the world [Savage 10]. The audience for comics grew to astounding proportions [Goulart 241].

After the war, however, interest in the superheroes began to wane. The atomic bomb was so overwhelming that costumed strongmen no longer seemed "super" to the American public. As a result, the comics' publishers started looking for new genres that would sell. Crime comics, western comics, war comics, and romance comics all started appearing. Like post-war Americans, comics had entered an age of complacency.

MLJ Publications started a back-up feature about "America's Typical Teenager"... a red-haired Romeo named Archie Andrews. Archie and his pals--Betty, Veronica, and Jughead--were America's stereotypical teenagers, sweet and carefree. They had typical 1950s concerns: finding dates, buying "cool" clothes, and getting Archie's jalopy to run. Archie eventually pushed all MLJ's superheroes off the stands, which showed how 1950s teens favored comics that reflected the lighthearted mood of their everyday lives.

At the same time, EC Publications (which Max Gaines had started after leaving DC and which was now being run by his son Bill) started grinding out horror comics [Daniels 79]. Clearly, they were catering to different audiences. With such titles as *Tales from the Crypt* and *Weird Science*, Bill Gaines and his crew set the industry scrambling in a new direction, one that eventually spawned a parental uproar and a Congressional investigation.

With each new rival publisher going for more and more gory material, it was an easy task for psychologist Fredric Wertham to blame all the ills of society on comic books. He gained notoriety and generated healthy sales of his book *Seduction of the Innocent*. Wertham's efforts spurred Congress to divert their attention briefly from Communism to the issue of juvenile delinquency. Congress viewed comics as a medium exclusively for children. Since the comics were very violent, they would therefore have to be altered to conform to Congress's narrow views of acceptable reading material [Daniels 83].

Congress's attempt to clamp down on comics reflects the general conservative attitude of the 1950s, the country's fear of "subversives" and strangers. Their "witch hunt" against comics is a variation of their "witch hunt" against Communists.

In an attempt to forestall Congressional action and public backlash, the larger publishers banded together and formed the Comics Magazine Association, with a Comics Code for appropriate comic book material. Like the blacklisted "Communists," Gaines and his competitors were forced to abandon comics virtually overnight. Gaines himself was called before the Senate Judiciary Subcommittee during the aforementioned hearings on juvenile delinquency. Gaines did, however, continue on the fringe of the business, publishing a highly successful comic book-turned-magazine to dodge the code: *MAD* [Daniels 85].

Comic books languished throughout the early and mid-50s until Julius Schwartz, an editor at DC in 1956, proposed bringing the superheroes back for another try. This was not a return to the escapism of the 1930s, though. These new heroes would be thoroughly modern--"more human," claimed the publishers. Schwartz revised and revamped DC's old lineup, including The Flash, Green Lantern, Hawkman, The Atom, and the Justice League of America [Crawford 326].

In part, these mythical heroes filled the need and desire for real heroes, a role filled by baseball players Joe DiMaggio and Jackie Robinson, movie stars John Wayne and Charlton Heston, and military figure Dwight David Eisenhower.

Meanwhile, over at Atlas (formerly Timely) Comics, publisher Martin Goodman saw the success of his rivals and suggested to his young editor that they should start publishing superhero comics as well. The editor, a longtime writer of comics for Timely/Atlas named Stan Lee, took a shot and created the Fantastic Four, Spider-Man, the Incredible Hulk, and the X-Men [Crawford 340].

It should be mentioned, however, that for many years these new superhero comics were not as reflective of American society as their predecessors had been. The early sixties saw almost as many new comic book characters as the 1940s had, but while 1940s heroes protected the homefront in World War II, 1960s heroes scarcely, if ever, mentioned Vietnam [Savage 66].

As the Vietnam War escalated, the popularity of war comics decreased, with the notable exception of comics that showed the gritty, unglamorous side of war. The DC comic *Enemy Ace*, for example, described World War I from the vantage point of a German pilot, thus humanizing the enemy. The previous generation of war comics, in contrast, had portrayed war from the soldier's point of view. The Sergeant Rock stories continued this new trend, focusing much more on human relations than on the patriotic spirit of World War II comics. By the end of the Vietnam War, the only war comic left was Sgt. Rock. But like any other old soldier, he eventually faded away.

In the early 1970s, DC had another brief period of historical relevance as the new generation of writers combined journalism with fiction. "Not fact, not current events presented in panel art, but fantasy rooted in the issues of the day," said Denny O'Neil, a comic author of that time, describing these new comics. These angry issues dealt with racism, overpopulation, pollution, and drug addiction. DC dramatized the drug abuse problem in an unusual and unprecedented way by showing Green Arrow's heretofore clean-cut boy sidekick Speedy turning into a heroin addict. These comics clearly show America's concern with the pressing social issues of the day. While DC was showered with praise for this bold move, declining sales caused Schwartz to announce in 1973, "Relevance is dead." [Goulart 297]

Also in the 1970s, the comic book industry became aware that their audience was changing. Instead of losing all its readers at age 14 (as had been the pattern in the past), they were staying on, looking for more diverse and challenging material. Coupled with the growth of a direct market, in which the publishers could supply books directly to specialized comic book shops, and the utilization of new printing technologies, the industry went through its largest expansion, with record numbers of titles being produced every month [Goulart 307]. As America became more open about previously taboo subjects--sex and violence--comics became much more gritty and realistic.

Today's comics deal with important issues on a new level. Timely/Atlas, now called Marvel Comics, dealt with racism in a whole new way. After they established that their heroes were "Mutants," they ran a crossover series about the mutant hate groups that had sprung up in the comic-book world. Cries of "Die Mutie scum!" echoed through the comics with an almost Ku Klux Klan-worthy fervor [Goulart 332].

A new generation of horror comics, many produced by fans-turned-professionals from England, began to appear, aimed at an adult audience. Far more graphic than those of the 1950s, but also with far more complex storylines, these books in particular have led former readers back into the comic book fold. This echoes the way television and movies have changed to fit the public's taste over the past forty years [Goulart 344]. DC's Vertigo line targets the same audience as the TV show *Buffy the Vampire Slayer*.

Over the years, as society as changed, so have comics. Now, as the world becomes increasingly computerized, comic companies have Web pages. In addition, most of the larger comic companies are coloring on computer rather than by hand. As the world continues to change, the comic book industry must continue to adapt to fit the needs and wants of its audience if it is to survive.

Works Cited

Crawford, Hubert H. *Crawford's Encyclopedia of Comic Books*. Middle Village, N.Y.: Comicade Enterprises, 1978.

Daniels, Les. *COMIX: A History of Comic Books in America*. New York: Bonanza Books, 1971.

Goulart, Ron. *Great History of Comic Books*. Chicago, Ill.: Contemporary Books, Inc., 1986.

Savage, William W. *Comic Books and America*, 1945–1954. Oklahoma: University of Oklahoma Press, 1990.

Thomson, Don. *The Comic-Book Book*. New Rochelle, N.Y.: Arlington House, 1973.

Model #2: Prozac: Salvation or Damnation?

Outline

Thesis: Prozac should be used with great care.

  I. Introduction
     A. Anecdotal opening
     B. Thesis
 II. Background
     A. How Prozac works
     B. Statistics on sale and use
III. Advantages of Prozac (opposition side)
     A. Emotional calm
     B. Fewer side effects than other antidepressants
     C. Helps many patients
 IV. Disadvantages of Prozac (writer's side)
     A. Side effects may outweigh advantages
        1. Thoughts of suicide
        2. Emotional void
        3. Decreased libido
        4. Personality changes
        5. May accelerate tumor growth
        6. Other side effects
     B. May be overprescribed
     C. Provides only a quick fix
  V. Conclusion

Prozac: Salvation or Damnation?

Melissa Ryder was suffering from depression. To relieve her symptoms, her doctor prescribed Prozac. "After only six days on Prozac, I was in far worse shape than I had ever been before," she said in an interview. Her bizarre side effects included dreams of bouncing off walls, uncontrollable trembling, urges to stab herself, and thoughts of killing her children. Melissa Ryder is no longer using Prozac and her condition has improved greatly [Bowe 42].

Despite Prozac's tremendous global popularity, some serious issues are being raised about its negative effects. Prozac's many side effects can do more damage than the makers of the drug could have ever imagined, as Melissa Ryder's case illustrates. While Prozac can help some people suffering from depression and other mental disorders, it should be used only with great care.

Prozac, also known by its chemical name Fluoxtine, is the first "designer drug" created expressly to treat depression by altering the biochemistry of only one system in the brain. Prozac interferes with the reabsorption process of serotonin going into the brain. It slows down the uptake of serotonin, making it more available to the brain when needed [Brown 153].

In 1993, the sale of Prozac totaled $1.2 billion. A one month's supply of the drug retails for approximately $63. Toward the end of the 1993, it was estimated that ten million people worldwide have taken Prozac [Breggin 47]. These figures show that Prozac must be helping many people.

The drug clearly has some advantages in the treatment of depression. Doctors boast that Prozac affords some patients a consistent, calm feeling, unlike that achieved through other antidepressants that have less severe side effects than Prozac. According to science writer Claudia Bow, "Prozac happens to have fewer side effects because it alters one brain chemical (serotonin), while most other antidepressants affect many chemical systems in the brain" (44).

Speaking of her depression, Margaret London, an office manager in Manhattan, said, "Everything was gray and black. It was like being in a pit." Ms. London tried all the different kinds of anti-depressants currently on the market, but only Prozac helped her. She said, "After being on Prozac, I began to realize that I no longer felt depressed and unhappy. I felt as if someone had whitewashed the world" [Bowe 42].

Although Prozac was beneficial to Margaret London, for many patients, Prozac's side effects greatly outweigh its benefits. Prozac's negative effects range from suicide to sexual dysfunction. Martin Teicher, a psychiatrist from Boston University, studied his patients on Prozac and concluded, "A significant percentage of Prozac users were thinking of stabbing themselves, turning on gas jets in their apartments and striking a match to blow themselves up" ["Open Verdict" 76]. Other psychiatrists have reported similar results. In September, 1989, a man taking Prozac shot twenty people and then killed himself. His doctor said that the man was not violent until he began taking Prozac. As a result of this incident, lawsuits amounting to hundreds of millions of dollars were filed against Eli Lilly, the company that sells Prozac ["Open Verdict" 76].

There are also complaints from people of feeling devoid of emotions while on Prozac. Dr. Randolph Catlin, a psychiatrist and chief of the mental health service at Harvard University, said, "Many of the students I treated with Prozac reported feeling split off from themselves. They felt as though they were not there any more." He added, "One wonders if these reports that you hear about patients acting aggressively while on Prozac might be cases where patients who are out of touch with their feelings act on their impulses, without having any feelings of guilt or concern" [Nichols 39].

Dulled or absent sexual response is a problem, too. It has been reported that some individuals on Prozac have a decreased libido or no desire for sexual activity. A United States study, published in *The Journal of Clinical Psychiatry* in April 1994, found that among 160 patients taking Prozac, 85 reported that their sexual desire or response diminished after using the drug [Nichols 36].

In addition, many patients on Prozac began to experience personality changes over time. A new study described at the annual meeting of the American Psychiatric Association suggests that Prozac alters aspects of personality as it relieves depression. Ron G. Goldman, a psychiatrist at Columbia University, believes that "Emotional and personality factors are intertwined in depression so it's not really surprising that some type of personality change would accompany improvement in this condition" [Bower 359]. Similarly, psychiatrist Peter Kramer, in his book *Listening to Prozac*, claims, "Prozac offers nothing less than self transformation, turning self-doubts into confidence, increasing energy, even improving one's business acumen" [94].

In other cases, doctors have reported side effects of a more serious nature. Some scientists suspect that Prozac may accelerate tumor growth in people who already have cancer. In July 1992, the journal *Cancer Research* published a paper by a group of researchers showing that tumors in mice and rats seemed to grow faster when the animals were given Prozac [Nichols 40].

Prozac's other reported unpleasant side effects include jumpiness, nausea, insomnia, unwanted weight gain, headaches, and rapid heartbeat. "These symptoms have appeared in hundreds of thousands of patients," said Peter R. Breggin, MD, author of "Another View: Talking Back to Prozac." He adds, "When a doctor prescribes Prozac, it should be understood that these symptoms exist and that the risk is quite high. I believe that these warnings go unsaid as millions of people continue to take Prozac" [Brown 153–55].

Prozac is now the most frequently prescribed psychiatric medication. Physicians, mostly non-psychiatrists, are now writing almost one million prescriptions a month for the drug. "Many medical experts worry that some doctors are over-prescribing Prozac and using it to treat relatively trivial disorders" [Nichols 36].

In addition to overprescribing, there are problems with using Prozac as a quick-fix remedy. Psychiatrist Peter Breggin, cited earlier, said,

"Too many doctors prescribe Prozac for minor depression or anxiety without talking to patients long enough to understand their problems. Too many patients look for pills to smooth out the inevitable ups and downs of everyday life" [Breggin 46-8]. Breggin argues, "In looking for the quick fix, too many psychiatrists have forgotten the importance of love, hope, and empathy in maintaining sanity." He adds, "The main problem is Prozac is merely a stimulant that does not get to the root of depression and is dangerous when used improperly" [Breggin 80].

Over time, Prozac's dark side is becoming more apparent to the medical community and eventually to the general public. Maybe Prozac isn't the wonder drug of the 90s. While Prozac may help some people, it is not a miracle cure.

Works Cited

Breggin, Peter. "Another View: Talking Back to Prozac." *Psychology Today*. July/August 1994: 46-81.

—— *Talking Back to Prozac*. New York: St. Martin's Press, 1994.

Brown, Avery. "Miracle Worker." *People Weekly*. November 15, 1993: 153-5.

Bowe, Claudia D. "Women and Depression: Are We Being Overdosed?" *Redbook*. March 1992: 42-4.

Bauer, Bruce. "Antidepressants May Alter Personality." *Science News*. June 4, 1994: 359.

Kramer, Peter. *Listening to Prozac*. New York: Penguin, 1993.

Nichols, Mark. "Questioning Prozac." *McLean's*. May 23, 1994: 36-41.

"Open Verdict: Prozac and Suicide." *The Economist*. January 19, 1991: 76.

Index